Banking

The root cause of the injustices of our time

Edited by: Abdalhalim Orr and
Abdassamad Clarke

DIWAN PRESS

Copyright © Diwan Press Ltd., 2009 CE/1430 AH

Banking: the root cause of the injustices of our time

Published by: Diwan Press Ltd.
                                 Unit 4, The Windsor Centre
                                 Windsor Grove
                                 London
                                 SE27 9NT
Website: www.diwanpress.com
E-mail: info@diwanpress.com

First edition: Abdalhalim Orr (Editor)
Second Edition: Abdassamad Clarke (Editor)
Typeset by: Abdassamad Clarke
Cover design "The Wasteland" by:
                                 Muhammad Amin Franklin
A catalogue record of this book is available from the British Library.

ISBN-13:   978-1-84200-110-3 (paperback)

Printed and bound by: Mega Basim

"…it has produced what the world never saw before; starvation in the midst of abundance."
William Cobbett (1763 – 1835)

Contents

Twenty Years After

THE TITLE "Twenty years after" refers to our taking stock of the situation since publication in 1989 of the proceedings of the original Norwich seminar, *Usury: root cause of the injustices of our time*. Rather suggestively, it also lends itself to the evocation of Alexander Dumas' book of the same name. In utterly brilliant fashion, Dumas sketches life in the 17th century French royal court, replete with its intrigues, liaisons and love affairs, usually inextricably interwoven. This occupies a good first third of the book as the reader is gradually drawn into the conspiracies and political game-playing when, quite suddenly, the author introduces into the story the now middle-aged but still heroic figure of D'Artagnan. The effect is astonishing, like the appearance of spring after a long winter, or a fresh wind after a long soporific summer of overcast weather and sultry storms.

For those of us fortunate enough to have attended the original seminar, it had exactly the same effect on us. After lifetimes of hearing the endless analyses of left and right, Conservatives and Labour, Democrats and Republicans, here was an argument that went to the core of the matter in one bound, and yet did so with a degree of scholarship, and indeed erudition, that was anything but cavalier. The result was electric. It was also well before its time.

However, with the catastrophic bank collapses of 2008 and the total systems shutdown of 2009, history has furnished us another opportunity to place this vital material before the reader. Whatever the result of these signal events – a slide into depression, cataclysmic upheaval or a rebound into dynamic activity – the argument in this work nevertheless stands: usury is demonstrably the motor of the injustices of our age.

Accepting that usury and its machinations have moved on considerably since the term was first coined as a euphemism for the charge made for the 'use' of money – we must also acknowledge that we are no longer talking about 'extortionate interest on a loan' as in modern dictionary definitions or even just plain 'interest on a loan' as in the etymological dictionaries, abhorrent though both these matters are, but we are now confronting the very nature of money itself.

That we have conceded to groups of utterly disreputable people the right to invent money out of nothing, and then to lend it to us, at their discretion, and at 'extortionate' interest rates is simply beyond belief. It is hardly credible that we, as human beings, could have been so gullible. Nevertheless, there we are. In the interim, many have pointed to this crime, and many have recommended cures for it, but unfortunately some of the alternatives have been even worse than the original crime.

It would take a leap of utter genius, childlike in its immediacy, such as that provided by Hans Christian Anderson's visionary tale *The Emperor's New Clothes*, to reach the perfectly obvious conclusion that we do not need the gold standard again, since that would have to be managed by the banks, whose ill-fitting sheep's clothing had fallen off once too often to hide the naked fangs of the wolves from whom we wished to escape. What we need is actual gold and silver themselves, and trade in real commodities without the interference of economists and financiers who, to a man, are steeped in the old usurious thinking.

That leap was achieved by Shaykh Abdalqadir as-Sufi, and it was taken to its furthest elaboration in both theory and practice by his student Umar Ibrahim Vadillo, whose works we wholeheartedly recommend to the reader since they introduce us to modes of trade and commerce that are in harmony with the rights of all peoples and the rights of the earth itself and its ecosystems and will remain so into the distant future being based upon natural rather than usurious parameters.

Much of the work in this book, whether from the seminar or the contemporary material, has been carried out by Muslim authors whose aim it has been to recover the values that lie at the core of the Judaeo-Christian and the classical Greek philosophical traditions that lie at the very root of everything that is Western culture. In contrast, spurious so-called 'Islamic economics' consists of a drive on the part of certain Muslim academics and interested financiers to recast modern usurious commercial instruments in such a way as to supply the resulting Muslim demand with an exclusive range of 'alternative' financial transactions. What this book proposes instead is the dynamic reactivation of the original commercial law of Islam which endorses the best of our common Western heritage and involves Muslims and non-Muslims transacting harmoniously with a shared set of non-usurious instruments.

The reader, whoever he or she may be, is invited to take this discovery and make use of it in the assurance that as well as having its roots in the Western tradition, it also formed the substance of non-usurious trade for an entire global civilisation involving Muslims, Christians, Jews and many others, for almost a millennium and a half until, with a number of honourable exceptions, they fell for the lure of the limitless wealth apparently offered by the bankers. Unfortunately, the combination of gullibility and sheer greed was enough to blind the majority to the realisation that the limitless wealth was based on limitless and exponentially expanding debt which, having been unleashed, has now come close to destroying the social and ecological equilibrium of the entire biosphere we call Earth.

A major change in the book since its first publication in 1989, apart from the addition of some new material, is to rename it *Banking: the root cause of the injustices of our time,* nevertheless acknowledging the inadequacy of the term 'banking' to cover fiat money, fractional reserve banking, the stock exchanges, credit-default-swaps, derivatives, hedge funds and the whole complex of instruments and institutions that is collapsing around our ears.

As to the new articles in the Postface, the first, *Crisis! What Crisis?,* was written in response to two eminent Anglican Archbishops' pontifications on the unfolding economic collapse. Its inclusion here is not accidental since the Church was in at the birth of the current world banking order, baptismal font at the ready. The second is the text of a speech by Dr. Zeno Dahinden to a conference in South Africa in which he outlined the 20th century history that has culminated in the events of 2008-9. The third, *Open Trade – A Call to Action,* is a summary of key elements of the way forward that, as well as being grounded in historical practice, is today being put into action by increasing numbers of people.

A hope is dawning, and many people are waking up to the falsity of the bankers' promises, so our wish is only that this work, though small, will be a sharp and ready tool that will provide the reader with the necessary inspiration to put it to its best use.

Abdassamad Clarke

Usury:

The Root Cause of the Injustices of Our Time

Norwich, UK 1987

Transcripts of the Seminar

Notes on the Seminar of 1987

This seminar was presented by a group of people who believe that usury is a crime against mankind, against nature, against life. We believe that it is at the root of the current disaster scenario facing us all, and that until it is confronted and eliminated, other issues cannot be adequately dealt with. They are branches – usury is a root.

The material was prepared during the three months preceding the seminar, and it should be stated that none of those involved was a "specialist" in this field. Everyone started – in essence – from scratch, from a belief, and with a determination to do something about what we see and experience around us.

The resultant material should not be viewed as an attempt to create a complete file on the subject matter, and it is therefore incomplete. This is not the point. The point is that this work is a demonstration that it does not need special people to undertake this task, – indeed it is up to us all as the people of this country to undertake it – and that if this seminar reopens the issue of the illegality of usury, a subject that has been debated heatedly at various times and places, then it will have been a success.

For the voices against usury have been effectively silenced. So effectively that most people do not know what it is, how it operates, who benefits by it and who suffers. As a result, the whole planet is in the stranglehold grip of interest-bearing debts and inherently worthless money, which if left unchecked, will squeeze the very life out of us all.

We are saying that it must stop. Completely.

Abdalhalim Orr

Introduction

FIRSTLY some explanation about the reasons for holding this seminar, and the meaning of its title may be necessary, but before I give this I would like to ask you to do something for us. You may have gathered from our names, or you may know from past acquaintance, that we, that is the presenters of this seminar, are Muslims. We ask you to put this aside, as what we are going to present to you today concerns us all, we are all members of this society and its commonly recognised problems are problems for us all.

We believe that what we are presenting here today is concerned with the continued existence of all of us in this society – possibly even about the survival of the human race. We in fact believe that being human is about behaviour, acting in a balanced, responsive and responsible way in our society.

Something which many of you here are familiar with, and which has become a hot issue, is the so-called "debt problem", usually associated with the "Third World". We wish to show that this is only one symptom of a sickness, an imbalance, in the economic life of this society, which affects us all, the oppressive nature of which is daily becoming more apparent through social and environmental destructiveness and political tyranny. We will attempt to show that there is a common root to all manifestations of this sickness – a mechanism in financial transactions that was once known as usury, in popular parlance "moneylending". We wish to reactivate a debate that was a major political and social issue throughout the fifteenth and sixteenth centuries, concerning what was just in economic dealings. We wish to show that usury is no more acceptable now than it was then, and how economic imperatives and technique of a particular kind are related to the destructive imbalances we see today.

Since usury is a term no longer in common use, we should begin by saying what it is. This is only a preliminary attempt at definition, as in practice it is subtle and can take many forms. We are still developing our own understanding of it – so! some definitions:

✳ It is usury to exchange a given amount of a particular commodity for any more or less than exactly the same amount of that same commodity, whether any delay is involved or not.

✳ It is usury to acquire gain from the use of a thing not in itself fruitful without there being any labour, expense or risk on the part of the lender.

✳ It is usury to stipulate taking back more than the principal in repayment of a loan.

✳ It is usury to make money directly out of money.

It is a characteristic property of usury that the gain from it is certain and automatic.

All of this can be loosely summed up by the phrase "obtaining something for nothing". It may be difficult at first sight to see how this can constitute a major cause of the injustices of our time, but its profound implications and innumerable ramifications will become increasingly apparent as the seminar progresses.

It is, however, important at this stage to note that the present commonly understood meaning of the word usury, that is that 'usury' is confined to extortion by means of exorbitant rates of interest, is not the correct definition and that the term 'usury' in fact covers the taking of any interest whatsoever. By the end of this presentation you will have a taste of the meaning of the term, and how it affects economy and society.

We hope that this seminar is only a beginning and that it might develop into an arena of understanding and political action.

Abdalhalim Orr

Where Does the Buck Stop?

WHAT WE WANT to do is to try and find out what has happened, what's gone wrong. How did we get to where we are?

Let us imagine that we are looking at the body of a crime victim. Multiple injury, heavy duty GBH, rape and robbery of an unprecedented nature. The victim's condition is serious, critical, but there is still life. It's not yet time for an autopsy, but it soon will be, if something is not done.

We have come across the scene of the crime, stumbled over the body, probably got some blood on our clothes. Naturally we are concerned, horrified, but what can we do? We could walk away, pretend we didn't see it, we weren't actually there. It's probably too much to deal with anyway. Can't handle it. Don't get involved.

Or we can accept responsibility for where we find ourselves. The victim is clearly in need; surely there is something that we can do, even if we are not experts.

The victim is the planet and its inhabitants, the people, animals plants, oceans, forests, the air, earth and water. Life itself.

But how did this happen, who did it, why? It's too awful to be an accident. How can we put it right? Can we put it right? The questions beg an answer.

One does not necessarily have answers, but let's at least try and understand what has taken place.

We do know that the official version of things, the story as we have been told it is highly suspect. It sounds very much like an alibi put out by the likeliest of suspects.

So let's try and start at the beginning. This may all sound rather simplistic, but we want to break down a complex affair into sizable bites, in order to digest it, and use it in a positive and intelligent manner.

We are dealing with something unnatural, a gross imbalance, something so out of sync at the centre, that it has thrown everything else out of step.

In trying to understand and cope with this global imbalance, it is tempting to look at the symptoms, because they are more manageable, and try and deal with it in that way. Let's save the whales, or the rain forests. Maybe concentrate on pollution, or the arms race, nuclear power, inner city crime.

These issues are all valid, but they are all symptoms of this extreme imbalance. They are the results of something, and if we only focus on them we may miss seeing the cause. For if we are to nurse the patient back to life we have to find the cause of the disease. How did the cancer start?

One could describe life as a series of transactions, some simple some complex. Chemical, personal, social, national, global, cosmic.

Endless exchanges and interactions. Planets spin, seasons shift, day turns into night.

And people buy and sell, they exchange things. It's probably the most basic human social transaction. Wherever there are people, it's going on. Everything you see has probably been bought, sold or exchanged.

It is a type of social bedrock.

Transactions are exchanges that are mutually beneficial, both parties gain from the exchange, it is part of social movement and growth. I give you this, you give me that, and we are both pleased with the exchange and everyone else can see that everything is OK. $2 + 2 = 4$. There is balance, equilibrium.

Things go wrong when someone wants something for nothing

$10 = 11$, $2+2=5$

One pound $+$ Gateway Building Society $=$ Three pounds.

In order for you to believe it, some sleight of hand will be needed.

Barter of one thing for another, goods for goods without the use of money is the obvious basis for trade, but from earliest times a medium of exchange has been found to be necessary. You may not have the goods I need, so if I swap my goods for money, the medium of exchange, I can get what I want.

This medium of exchange must be something of actual value in itself, you are converting your goods into this other thing, this medium, in order to exchange that in turn for what you want. Why would anybody change their goods for something worthless? Would you? You're kidding! My goods represent a lot of my time and energy and sweat, they are worth something, they are real, valuable, they improve the quality of your life, they're useful. Why should I swap them for something of no value? The idea is ridiculous!

And yet this is exactly what we all do, every day.

The medium of exchange is a third element in the equation, or you can almost say it's like the = sign in maths. This table equals these chairs. Or the table equals £50 equals the chairs.

This does not mean that the price of my goods or your goods are not subject to normal fluctuations. That's OK. The price may go up and down, it can be 40 or 60 pounds, but the value of the POUND must remain a constant, or we don't know what £50 means. Then we're all in trouble, we don't know where we stand. It's no longer bedrock, it's quicksand. The medium of exchange must have intrinsic value of its own, it must be worth something. This is a necessary element of social stability.

It is pivotal, and if you change it, you change every transaction, like shifting the fulcrum on a set of scales.

Gold and silver are the obvious choices. They have value, their nature does not change even over long periods of time, they don't decay. They can be split up into lots of small pieces, and then put back into big ones again. They fit the bill, and historically, they have been used with great success.

Ah, yes, that's all very well, they say. But there's only so much gold, what if there isn't enough to go round, supposing it runs out?

Well, lets think about this for a bit. The fact is everything else in existence is finite, there is only so much of anything. There is a limited amount of all of our resources as we are finding out to our concern. There is only so much. This is fine until we get to modern economics.

Modern economics is based on continual growth, endless expansion, it will all keep getting bigger and better, more profits. This idea is now very deeply rooted and, as we shall see, it is very closely linked to the whole concept of Progress. Development. To disagree with the idea of endless growth is like saying you're against progress. You want to turn the clock back, put us all back in the dark ages.

Growth is part of life, it is delightful. Endless growth becomes grotesque.

An international banker was recently asked what he thought was wrong with the world economy, and he said "We need more growth."

This premise of constant growth defies every natural law in existence, it's like trying to deny the law of gravity. What goes up does not keep going up. We don't have endless day, nonstop summer. The wheel turns, there is expansion and contraction, profit and loss.

So, let us, like others have done for thousands of years, accept that a stable medium of exchange with intrinsic value of its own is an integral part of a balanced economy, which is in turn an essential part of a just society. I think that this is a reasonable starting place.

Modern economics is regarded as some kind of specialist subject, it has its own special language. But specialised knowledge should not be necessary to understand something that we all take part in on a day to day basis. The chances are that we all use money everyday. The monetary structure involves us all. In fact it limits us, contains us, we are all subject to its established rules. And if it is unjust, it enslaves us, it traps us. And once trapped, we can be controlled.

And this is actually the crux of the matter. We are proposing that the current economic system, that is now of global proportions, has ensnared all of us. It is unjust, immoral, and highly dangerous. It is like a massive spider's web, spun by the ultimate consumers, and we are all caught in it.

The monetary system is really a control mechanism.

The basis of the system is usury, and I'm using the word in a broad sense. Usury as a principle. Later on we will examine the historical picture of what events actually took place, but what I want to do here is outline the process whereby money became valueless and unreal. And hand in hand with this process there has developed a network of global banks, markets, and communications, a System, that has permitted those with wealth to get increasingly rich and powerful, and has forced pretty much everybody else, including those of us in the developed countries, into something that approaches slavery. This process has permitted the scale of imbalance that we are now talking about ... and experiencing.

What's usury?

Well, two key principles are: interest and unreal money.

1. Charging interest on loans of real money, gold.

2. Creation of paper money, i.e. promissory notes, as currency even when backed by gold.

3. Charging interest on loans of paper (unreal) money

4. Creating money out of nowhere, i.e. not backed by gold.

5. Creating paper money

6. Plastic money

7. Electronic money

8. Stock markets

9. Futures contracts

10. Eurobonds, etc.

11. Commodity speculation

These are the weapons, the instruments.

Funnily enough, you hear people talk about real money, I'd like to get my hands on some REAL money, you know, none of this small stuff, BIG money. They are referring to something almost non-existent, on the very edges of the physical world. That real money is nothing more than quivering electronic signals that get sent from one computer to another. Meta physics.

Yet everyone believes in it, accepts it as real and valuable. Anyone in a position to create this unreal wealth, to manipulate it, turn it into real wealth, weapons, land, energy, is in a position of great power. And that degree of power surely corrupts.

I am including all of these techniques and instruments as usury, because they all apply the same principle, and are all branches with the same root.

Without these economic tools, it would not be possible to have industry on a scale that causes global pollution, you couldn't build nuclear weapons or power stations, no star wars, no global destruction at the push of a button. You could not enslave a nation by market manipulation, in order to bleed their resources.

It simply could not be done.

Projects of such enormous size need huge financial backing. No individual, or group has enough real wealth to develop and build a fleet of F-11 fighter planes, let alone to finance the star wars programme. Without the help of the banks, and all that funny money.

You couldn't destroy the Amazon rain forest, or pollute an ocean. The concepts themselves are amazing!

Mega projects require mega bucks. And as we shall see, the opposite is also true. These huge amounts of unreal money, all on deposit at attractive rates of interest urgently and desperately need the mega projects. The show must go on.

Let's go back to our gold economy. We used to buy and sell for gold and silver, gold and silver coins were the currency. And it worked. And not just on a small localised scale, as we'll see later. It worked if everyone held to the principles.

The trouble starts with the ones who want something for nothing. Here we can see the roots of the crime.

1. Lending gold out on interest. Even if it's real money, it's not acceptable, because it opens a door that must be kept shut. You borrow 10 and have to pay back 11. On a small scale I can see that you might say that there's not much wrong with it, and I agree that perhaps, on the face of it, it does not look like the crime of the age. But let's be patient, and see where we can go down this corridor, once the door has been opened. Because we are not talking theory. All this has actually happened, and somehow we have got to where we are, and we are not happy about it. This is the road we have taken.

Lending on interest allows the one with money to make more money, simply because he has it in the first place. It puts the lender in a strong position and the borrower in a weak position. Being in debt is bad enough, without having to repay more than you borrow. If a group of these lenders get together, start working as a team, that gives them power over the rest of their society. There's no doubt that the lender has the edge on the borrower.

The amazing thing is that usury was outlawed by almost everybody, in virtually every civilisation and society you look back at, it was against the law. Including England, until very recently. And yet it is now difficult for people to imagine life without it, no interest, no paper money. A thorough job has been done.

2. The next thing that happens is the promissory note. "I promise to pay the bearer on demand the sum of...". Its easy to imagine the origins. Sure, I'll lend you some gold, but why bother taking the gold. It's here locked away safe and sound. I'll give you a note that says I've lent you the money, you can use that instead. Everyone knows me, it's as good as gold! You can pay your rent or whatever it is, and then THAT person can come and collect the gold. Why carry it around?

That's a picture of what became a bank, issuing paper against gold reserves, in equal proportions, 1 for 1, a pound's worth of gold, a pound's worth of paper. So the door has opened a little wider, we've taken a distinct step away from our bedrock transactions.

Running parallel with this were the markets. As trade increased and became international, agents of the wealthy merchants would travel around. Someone would make a purchase of some goods and pay with a Bill of Exchange that could be exchanged for gold with the merchant who issued it. These bills began to be used to make other purchases, rather than being cashed in. They were used as currency. As differences began to occur in the exchange rates, some bills were worth more than others, and a market developed for the bills themselves.

You can see how this opens the way for the scenario where someone eventually takes the bill back to the original merchant, to find that he's gone bust, died, disappeared. So much for your piece of paper, suddenly it's not worth what you thought it was, you have been cheated, it's not fair.

Now, the people who control the money tend to be in charge. Traditionally power was in the hands of the Ruler or King, someone who was recognisably in command, everyone knew who he was, and even if it was a bit corrupt, or the currency got debased, it was all on a small scale, it was limited.

But as we shall see later, power and financial control were taken, bit by bit, out of the hands of the traditional rulers, and put in the hands of the merchants, and the bankers. And as trade became international, so international currency emerged, and an international monetary system developed. And with the emergence of this system, the seat of power became hidden, to the point where now no one really knows who is in charge.

One of the high-water marks in the development of this global network came in 1944, when all of the world's currencies were linked together. They were all tied in a fixed relationship to the dollar, and the dollar was itself tied to gold, $35 to the ounce.

For the first time ever, a global monetary system had been established that tied all of the world's major currencies, and by extension, all of the people who used them, into a unified structure, with its own rules and governing bodies, that completely bypassed the visible channels of government. Politics had become theatre, something to show on the 9 o'clock news. And it was all done so neatly, that for the most part no one noticed. But if the money was in your pocket, the chances were you were in someone else's.

So, to recap, we are outlining a development that has taken place whereby we have gone from real money, gold and silver, to something that was merely representative of real value. Something that had no actual value itself, but you could swap for the real thing. This was really the first step away from bedrock. It is one step removed, maybe not a huge one, because the paper was still tied to something precious, something of real value. But a very significant step nonetheless, because promising to do something and actually doing it are not the same thing, and its dangerous to think that they are.

The next step was the creation of money that was completely worthless. One of the problems with promissory notes is that if you print too many of them, you may not be able to keep your promises. If there are more bits of paper than there are bits of gold, you are in trouble. Supposing everyone wants to cash them in?

Clearly if this is your situation, you have to find a way to make the paper more attractive than the real thing.

The obvious way is through Interest.

This was really very clear with the situation of the dollar in the 50's. The dollar was very strong, internationally accepted pretty much everywhere in the world. And if you had some you could put them in the bank and they would earn interest, the money would go to work for you, give you that little bit extra. If you could get enough, maybe you wouldn't have to go to work at all. It was a very attractive idea.

Gold on the other hand was not nearly so fertile, it didn't grow, no one gave you interest for it, in fact you had to pay to keep it somewhere safe.

The dollars were altogether better.

Unless there start to be too many of them.

Imagine the temptation. You are all set up with the printing presses, you can print as much money as you like, really. It's not against the law … you made sure of that. And there are all these things you want to do, all these things to buy, nice foreign goods, tasty bits of real estate, a bit of influence here and there. Well, let's print a few more and go and do it. It's hard to imagine anyone being able to resist such a temptation. Instant money. Influence. Success. And of course, power.

The system however, was not without flaws. All those dollars for example, and all of them theoretically convertible to gold. And when the potential demands on the gold became too great, the dollar was finally cut loose from the gold standard by President Nixon, in 1971, and the dollar, with all the other currencies in tow, started to drift free, blown on the turbulent winds of the market place.

And bedrock is now starting to look rather far away.

To further aggravate matters, the sharp and dramatic rises in the price of oil, and the incomprehensibly large amounts of money that this produced, only made things worse.

Staggering sums of money, the petrodollars, began to be put on deposit in banks round the world, all earning a nice bit of interest. But this created a real problem, because this money had to be put out to work by the banks in order to make enough to pay the depositors. And the best way to make money is to lend it out at a higher rate of interest than you're paying.

And the bigger the deposits, the bigger the loans have to be, and the riskier they are likely to become.

Once the concept of worthless money had been totally accepted by everyone without so much as a murmur, it was not difficult to bring some other tricks out of the hat. The audience was nicely warmed up, and it looked like they'd buy pretty much anything.

Like Eurodollars.

Simply put, these are dollars that are totally outside the American banking system. They don't belong anywhere, and they owe allegiance to no one. And they are completely free of the normal banking restrictions, they are not controlled at all. And they were great for business.

Now, the Federal Reserve requires US banks to put up a portion of their deposits as reserves to cover loans, and they can govern the character and size of the loan.

They say that if the bank gets a deposit of 100, it has to hold on to 10% as reserve, and can loan out the other 90. We go in and borrow that 90, and put it in our bank. That bank has to hold on to 9 and can lend out 81 to someone else, who puts it in his bank, who lend out 72.90 and so it goes on. Money coming out of nowhere.

In itself a pretty good trick.

But not Eurodollars. These can be deposited lent and repaid with no restrictions whatsoever. For every 100 dollar deposit, the banks can make a 100 dollar loan, each time. All with interest. Remember, here we are not even talking about paper money, its not MONEY in any previously accepted sense of the word, it's now electronic signals flickering through space, reproducing wildly as they go.

And our bedrock transaction is a speck of dust vanishing into the distance.

This means that if you are in the business of lending money, you can make an astronomical amount of money, and once you have astronomical amounts, you can make even more. 2 astronomical amounts, 3, 5, 100, just buy a bigger computer to keep track of the zeros.

For the bankers, the privately wealthy, the big corporations, this was the ultimate system. Once you had a certain amount, you could put it on deposit somewhere and scoop in the interest. Just because you had a lot, you could make a whole lot more.

But even if the money has now escaped the laws of gravity, nothing else has, everything else is still rooted in the finite universe, and there is only so much to go round. And if one man has a lot, then lots of people have to have a little.

All that fantasy money built great industrial vacuum cleaners, that hoovered up the resources of the rest of the world. And built new gadgets with the resources that were sold back to the third world, for them to buy with money lent to them by the same people who ripped them off in the first place.

It's all very neat.

The fantasy money gives real power to the ones who control it, because everyone believes in it. The paper money is in fact worthless, the banks are in fact virtually empty. But the game of musical chairs goes on, and as long as we all don't try and sit down at once, everything should be OK. It is a belief system, and it must be maintained at all costs if the status quo is to be preserved.

But no one dares to look too far upstream to see what's coming, because the idea of the system collapsing is too awesome to entertain.

But surely as day follows night, contraction must follow expansion, and the longer it's held at bay, the bigger the bang.

It is as if we have all been hypnotised, it's as if a spell has been cast over the planet. Borrow and spend, borrow and spend, everywhere you go, the message bombards you. Everyone is in debt, nations are in debt, babies are born into debt, even the lenders are all in debt to each other.

And the lenders tell the borrowers what to do, they control them, and dictate the terms. If you can't repay, we'll take your car, your house, your land, resources, your country. We'll put in our man, to make sure he keeps up the interest payments. If he doesn't, we'll kick him out and put in someone who will. Don't subsidise the bread to keep it affordable for the poor, put the price up and keep making the interest payments.

Or else.

I mentioned earlier that these huge amounts of money need these huge projects, like building massive dams in India, or cutting down the rain forests.

If, as a banker, I have taken 100 from you and am promising you say 10% interest, I have got to put that money to work, to make that extra 10 so you can have it when you come back and ask for it. The best way to make money is to lend it out at a higher rate of interest to someone else. This is the safest way.

But if I've taken billions of dollars on deposit, I've got to find someone with a real mega project up their sleeve, looking for some mega bucks.

Urgently. I've got to find it. Supposing you want your money back. And if I can't find someone who is already looking for this kind of money, then I'd better get out there and talk someone into wanting it. And here we have the whole myth of development. The politics of progress. Don't be backwards, don't just scratch around in the dirt, growing enough food to feed yourselves and live in peace. Get yourselves together. Get into the Space Age.

Just look at what could be yours.

And in order to do this you need to buy all this stuff.

And you need to buy it with dollars, real money.

Don't have any?

OK, what CAN you do? Enough of all this subsistence farming, and hunter gatherer business, you need a cash crop, something you can sell on the world market and get some real money.

You don't have what it takes to set that up?

Well you will have to borrow it, at the going rate of interest, you can pay it back later when you've got on your feet a bit more. It will all work out.

To make it all viable you'll need more arable land? Well let's cut down that big old forest over there for a start, you can use that, and you can build some dams to generate power, and you're going to need lots of cement and tractors, and why not have some TVs and stereos too. Might as well have some fun with all of this building going on. I'll bet you've got some handy resources and minerals you can sell too, once you're set up for it. We could probably take them off your hands.

We all know the scenario.

Then they sell you some weapons so you can protect yourself ... or is it so they can protect their investment?

Once you're tied into a scheme like that there's no easy way out. You will always be in debt, you'll just keep paying interest, wondering where it all went wrong.

But, the point is that the money is burning a hole in the banker's pocket, he's got to keep it moving, investing and lending to bigger and bigger projects and schemes. And every time he turns round there's even MORE money looking for somewhere to go. Remember endless growth? He's hustling like mad to invent more fantasy projects to use up all the fantasy money.

And ecological balance is a luxury the banker cannot afford. It's not even on his list. He needs short term gain, not long term balance. The System must survive. So what if some people get displaced, you lose a few seals, or there's a bit of pollution somewhere? Maybe cleaning up the mess will turn out to be big business, maybe he can make some investments in that.

He is a slave to his own system, his machine is running him. He has to keep the money rolling over, keep it on the move. It's essential, it's a ruthless, driving motivation. It's like the dot on the TV screen, if it keeps moving at the right speed, everyone will get the picture, the illusion works. If it stops, everything crumbles.

For it is really, in essence, a belief system. It all works because everyone believes in it. Believes in the money, the banks, the personalities, the politics, the promises and the lies. And all that belief gives them power.

The money is worthless, the banks are empty, we are all being cheated. And really they are not in control at all, and the great system contains within it the seeds of its own destruction.

For those of us who choose life, rather than anti-life, the question is not so much "What shall we put in its place?"

Rather, we must decide what tools we need, given the current scenario, that will enable us to cope with what we have inherited.

Meanwhile, back at the scene of the Crime, the victim is losing blood, losing consciousness. Species of life are disappearing from earth at a rate of nearly one an hour. If we were looking for a sign that all is not well, we could hardly ask for a more eloquent one than that.

Abdalhamid Evans

The History of Usury

"Take not usury nor more than thou gavest. Fear thy God, that thy brother may live with thee. Thou shalt not give him thy money upon usury nor exact of him any increase of fruits."

"Thou shalt not lend upon usury ... usury of money, usury of victuals or usury of anything that is lent upon usury."

"And if a man hath not lent upon usury nor taken increase he is just."

THESE THREE Old Testament quotes from Leviticus, Deuteronomy and Ezekiel respectively, and they are representative of several more, show that the prohibition of usury goes right to the legal and ethical roots of European civilisation. The prohibition was confirmed and even strengthened by the early Christians. St. Augustine for instance, who defined usury as occurring when a person expects to receive anything more than he has given, held usury to be so forbidden that any profits gained by it could not even be given away as charity. St. Thomas Aquinas was still continuing this position with clarity and vigour in the 14th century.

In the classical tradition, we find usury categorically dealt with by Aristotle. He said that of all the kinds of trade, the most unnatural and most justly hated is usury. Usury not only seeks an unnatural end, but misuses money itself, for money was intended to be used in exchange, not to increase at usury. Usury is the unnatural breeding of money from money. When we add to this the condemnation of Plato, who noted that usury inevitably set one class against another and was therefore destructive to the state, and that of the Roman philosophers Cicero, Cato and Seneca, we see that both the Judaeo-Christian and Graeco-Roman traditions, which together comprised the main sources of European civilisation, were unanimous on this issue. Religious and secular tradition spoke with one voice.

Thus it can be seen that the practice of usury had been subject to prohibition from ancient times. To put this down to primitivism, naivety and lack of economic understanding, which many detractors did and continue to do, is arrogant and a convenient way of side-stepping the underlying intellectual issues involved. The basis of the prohibition was ethical and theological and as such was concerned with deeper issues than economic expediency and international trade. Intrinsic to the prohibition of usury was the understanding that the essence of the usurious transaction – being guaranteed to get something for nothing – constitutes a rupture of natural law and is therefore bound to result in imbalance and disintegration. Any inconvenience incurred on the level of commercial transaction was put aside in favour of the larger consideration of the overall public good.

This does not mean to say that no transactions involving usury took place. They did. Very early on, the ancient Jews had claimed a scriptural licence to practice usury and the conditions under which they claimed to be allowed to do so give us a profound insight into the real nature of the usurious transaction. Deuteronomy Chapter 23 verse 20 states: "Unto a stranger thou mayest lend upon usury, but unto thy brother thou shalt not lend upon usury." The word "stranger" in this text is generally interpreted as "enemy" and armed with this text, the Jews used usury as a weapon, finding in it a means of gaining power over their enemies. By means of usury, other people's need could be transformed into their subjection.

From ghettos in the larger cities of Christendom, Jewish money-lending activities were carried on throughout the "Dark" and "Middle Ages". They were allowed to continue under strict scrutiny and were tolerated by the authorities only for as long as they were seen to provide a useful service. Even in this oppressive situation it was possible for the moneylender to gain enormous wealth by the practice of usury – Isaac of Norwich, for example. At one stage in 13th century England nearly half of the country's tax revenue was collected from the Jewish community who represented less than 5% of the population – but they were never able to turn their wealth into power, being subject to frequent and terrible popular purges, which in this country, resulted eventually in their expulsion from the country in the 14th century not to return for 350 years.

Money lending continued to exist on a small scale throughout the Middle Ages. Unscrupulous local merchants would take advantage of humble people who had got into difficulties by reason of a bad harvest or mismanagement or some other misfortune and would be forced to borrow to fulfil the ordinary necessities of life. In these cases there would usually be an attempt to conceal the usurious nature of the loan and if it did come to light, the usurer was subject to heavy penalties and became a social outcast.

Another area in which usury existed was right at the other end of the social scale. Kings and princes would raise enormous loans at interest, generally to finance some military expedition. These loans were usually raised from foreign sources, frequently Italian, and were paid by means of taxation, escaping by sheer size from the general prohibition.

However, to all intents and purposes, usury was completely excluded from all normal commercial and social transactions. It was like prostitution, known to exist but universally condemned and reviled as were those who practised it. In this atmosphere it was impossible for it to gain hold and, so long as the status quo in Europe remained unchanged, this attitude continued to prevail. However, starting with the Italian Renaissance in the 15th century things started to happen to gradually undermine the traditional order and they reached a head when on 31st October 1517, Martin Luther nailed his 95 theses to the church door in Wittenberg and the Reformation had begun. The repercussions of his challenge to the authority of Rome, went far beyond his apparent intention of reforming a corrupt institution. By his action he did more than any invading army had ever been able to do, he destroyed the unity of Western Christendom. His intention had been to break down the barriers between the individual and God; the actual result was to open the way to unlimited individual freedom of action. By breaking loose from Rome, he cast people adrift from the anchor of traditional morality which had been held in place by the Church's Canon Law, part of which was, of course, the complete prohibition of usury. The Catholic Church, in spite of all its deviation and corruption, nevertheless represented an unbroken tradition leading back to the teaching of Jesus and before him Moses. When its authority was broken by the Reformation, it was inevitable in the freer atmosphere of Protestantism that the binding strictures on usury would be cast off.

This occurred, significantly, through the unlikely means of the rigorous Puritan moralist Calvin. Whereas before this the entire matter of usury had been subject to a whole body of traditional, time-honoured doctrine, he treated the ethics of money-lending as a particular case among the general problems confronting human society which had to be solved in the light of existing circumstances. In other words he took the law into his own hands. He arrogantly dismissed the passages on usury in the Old Testament and the judgements of the past as irrelevant in the light of the prevailing circumstances and, arguing that taking interest on capital is as reasonable as taking rent for land, he opened the sluice gates to a flood which has since inundated the entire world. He took it upon himself to legalise the lending of money at interest, thus giving the sanction of the law to a practice that had been held to be illegal since earliest times. The fact that he allowed only moderate interest and hedged his indulgence round with strict qualifications made no difference. The merchant now had a precedent from someone who spoke with religious authority. According to Calvin the moral law had changed and therefore it was no longer immoral to charge interest. From then on the argument within the business community was not whether interest should be permitted, but how much.

From the Puritan atmosphere of Calvin's Geneva we move to the more salubrious goings-on at the court of Henry VIII in London. Henry had become extremely attached to one of his wife's maids-of-honour, one Anne Boleyn, and was determined to marry her. The Pope refused to annul his first marriage, being very reluctant to cross the powerful Emperor Charles V whose younger daughter, Catherine, was Henry's wife, and under Canon Law no other way of dissolving the marriage existed. So Henry, who, in his idealistic youth had earned the Pope's approval and the title "Defender of the

Faith" for his denunciation of Martin Luther, proceeded to follow Luther's example by breaking with Rome and declaring himself Head of the Church in England.

Not being by any means so scrupulous as those in whose footsteps he followed, he did not hesitate to take as much advantage as possible from the new situation. The licence that he proceeded to take in matrimonial matters is notorious. It is less well-known, though infinitely more important in historical terms, that one of his first actions was, following on from Calvin's precedent, to raise a loan from City merchants at the rate of ten per cent per annum, which rate was fixed as the limit for moderate interest, thus putting the seal of royal and religious approval on usury in England.

However, it must not be thought that the ancient prohibition was set aside without a voice being raised. A furious debate on the subject raged for well over a century. Many treatises and pamphlets were written and countless sermons and speeches given. One cleric in an ironic mood, said on the subject, "This hath been the general judgement of the Church for above this fifteen hundred years, without opposition, in this point. Poor silly Church of Christ that could never find a lawful usurie before this golden age wherein we live." The Frenchman Bodin, whose authority on economic matters was above question and who had no ecclesiastical axe to grind bluntly reasserted the traditional position when he said, referring to Calvin: "Those who maintain under the cover of religion that moderate usury of four or five percent is just, because the borrower gains as much as the lender, go against the Law of God which forbids usury absolutely and cannot be revoked." But none of this was able to really impinge on the course events were inexorably taking.

The situation was in some ways comparable to the nuclear debate in our own time. None of the passionate views expressed for or against nuclear disarmament in the public arena has any real effect on whether nuclear arms are manufactured and deployed for the simple reason that the decisions concerning these things are made in another sphere altogether and public opinion has no bearing on it one way or the other. So it was also with the introduction of usury. The source of political power had changed and the guardians of morality no longer had any real access to it.

Eventually, of course, the Churchmen themselves capitulated, and compromised rather than appear ridiculous – the Church of England has always been prone to the philosophy of "If you can't beat them join them." They officially redefined usury to fit in with normal business practice. It was now only usury to charge extortionate rates of interest and exactly what constituted an extortionate rate of interest was not clearly defined: so to all intents and purposes businessmen had a completely free rein. Whereas previously business practice had been subject to the moral law, now the moral law could be altered by business practice.

The general trend of the ultra-pragmatism of Tudor England, was briefly interrupted, though in the long run encouraged, by the accession of Henry's eldest daughter, Mary. Mary, whose mother was Catherine of Aragon, daughter of the Catholic Emperor Charles V, proceeded to marry her first cousin, the fanatical Catholic Philip, King of Spain, and was appalled at everything that her father had done. She reacted with extreme harshness, instituting an inquisition and burning alive many of those who had taken an active part in the breach from Rome. When her comparatively brief reign came to an end, there was a counter-reaction which enabled the pragmatist and mercantile elements to considerably increase their influence in the return to Protestantism during the reign of her half-sister Elizabeth.

I would at this point like to take a break from the historical continuum and briefly look at an aspect of English life that was being thoroughly affected by the relaxing of the laws of usury and the easy availability of credit that that made possible.

From ancient times most of the people in England had lived on and from the land. Although many of the more rigorous aspects of the Norman-imposed feudal system were no longer enforced, the situation remained much as it had been for several hundred years.

There were the great landed families with vast estates, usually divided into manors and squire-archies underlying all of which was the basic pattern of village life. Land was farmed in strips on an open field system. There were yeoman farmers who owned their own strips or leased them from the local landowner on a permanent basis, but the majority of village people were copyholders which meant that they had a traditional right to a certain amount of land for themselves in return for doing a certain amount of work and giving a certain amount of produce to their landlord. Apart from this cultivated land, there was also an area of common land where all had a right to graze their own livestock.

With the Tudors, certain changes to this traditional picture started to take place. Henry VII wanted to centralise power and extend his direct control to all parts of the country. One of the ways he did this was to elevate the merchant class who were based in the bigger cities and encourage them to become land owners, thus breaking up the land monopolies of the great aristocratic families. This process continued under Henry VIII and was given added impetus when he seized and sold the Church land during the dissolution of the monasteries, the main beneficiaries being the new class of landowners.

At the same time the nobility were encouraged to leave their estates and spend more time at Court in London. The upkeep of large establishments in London as well as the country together with the extravagance and expense entailed by court life led many courtiers to experience severe cash flow problems. Since it had now become much easier, in the light of the previously mentioned developments, to borrow money at interest, the needy courtier would approach a likely merchant who would usually be only too willing to accommodate him, taking as security for the loan the deeds to a manor or two on the courtier's estates. In this way many estates began to be encumbered by debt and when, as frequently happened, the nobleman defaulted, the manor held as security would pass into the possession of the merchant money-lender.

Up to this time, wealth and power had been inextricably bound up with the mere fact of ownership of land. The new landowners, whether they had got hold of their land by purchase, grant, or default, were not interested in feudal rights and responsibilities, but only in income, and therefore, increased production, and because of their debts even the old landowners themselves were now having to increase the income from their estates if they wanted to avoid losing them to their creditors. The traditional open field system was not a farming method that encouraged the increased production that was being sought and in the interests of greater economic efficiency came "enclosure". The enclosure movement probably had more effect on more people in terms of how they lived their everyday lives than anything else before or since. The old open fields where everyone had farmed strips according to their landholding or traditional right were divided up and enclosed by hedges, walls, dykes or whatever was appropriate, and in most places the common land suffered the same fate.

The result for the poorest section of society, the copyholders, who were by far the largest in terms of numbers, was catastrophic. Until this time they had been basically self-sufficient, farming their strips and grazing their few livestock on the common land, but all this was only by common consent and they were not able to prove any legal claim to the land they used.

Consequently great numbers of them were forced to leave their villages and seek their living in town and cities, becoming a captive work force for the incipient industrial revolution.

Even many small freeholders were forced off the land because they were not able to afford to carry out the necessary measures involved in enclosing land. Some of them stayed on to become tenant farmers and paid rent to farm the same land they had once owned outright.

Since the expense incurred in enclosing land, entailing as it did hedging, banking, ditching, draining, the resiting of buildings and roads and many other things, was considerable, very few landlords were able to meet them from their own resources. Once more enter the usurer, who was very willing to lend money at interest on the security of these land improvement schemes.

Thus we see that money lenders and money lending are not only a major cause of this momentous change in land use which completely altered the life and shape of the English countryside but also continued to benefit from its outcome, gaining enormous wealth without risk at the expense of the entire livelihoods of a considerable section of the population.

I have gone into this in some detail because it highlights clearly what happens when usury becomes widespread in any situation. Firstly there are far-reaching and irreversible economic and social changes. Secondly the benefit in the situation is channelled to an élite group at the expense of the poor and weak who become worse off, suffering increasing deprivation and hardship.

We left our historical narrative with Good Queen Bess, and good she certainly must have seemed to the Merchant Venturers and financiers who had gained so much influence during the Tudor period. Not so good perhaps to the copyholders dispossessed of their land by the enclosures. Certainly the most significant effect of Tudor rule as far as history is concerned was the shift that occurred in the balance of power away from the traditional power structure of the landed nobility towards a new élite drawn from the merchant class, the basis of whose power was financial wealth, which was increasing exponentially due to the employment of financial techniques whose use had previously been forbidden.

Elizabeth was succeeded by her second cousin James Stuart,

King of Scotland. James and his son Charles who was king after him, while they were not actually Catholics, definitely represented the old order. The doctrine of Divine Right they are famous for was not merely the arrogant assumption of power it is frequently portrayed as being, but implied responsibility on the part of the monarch to uphold the traditional moral order enshrined in the Canon Law. This, of course, ran contrary to the new spirit of mercantilism which tended to identify itself with the freedom from authority associated with the more extreme kinds of Protestantism. The mercantile class were strongly represented in Parliament and the latent hostility between the monarchy, which was desirous to restore the status quo, and Parliament, which felt that its recently acquired power was under threat, eventually erupted in the Civil War. Plato's observation about usury had proved itself to be true. Society had become divided against itself.

When Charles I was executed, a decisive blow was struck. It was a historical watershed. Power had changed hands. The old order had given way to the new.

Ironically it was the Puritan revolution which broke the mechanism whereby religious values were able to make themselves felt in political and legal terms and which ushered in the secular state. The science of ethics became divorced from its roots in revealed texts and became something to be decided by philosophers and legislators according to the fashions and needs of the time. Mercantilism and finance rapidly began to play a greater and greater role in government.

Cromwell had been forced to resort to Dutch as well as native financiers to pay for his military exploits, which included, apart from the Civil War itself and the notorious Irish expedition, a war against the Dutch. This, the first Dutch War, was the first war fought out of purely commercial considerations and shows how trade was beginning to take centre stage in political terms. It also demonstrated rather cynically that financiers stand to gain from war whatever side they are on. In the light of all this, it is significant, though not altogether surprising, that it was during this time that banking, which was in fact the institutionalisation of usury and the way it achieved complete respectability, began to take shape in the form it retains to this day.

The Earl of Clarendon was to write a few years later: *"Bankers were a tribe that had risen and grown up in Cromwell's time and never even heard of before the late troubles, till when the whole trade of money had passed through the hands of the scriveners: they were for the most part goldsmiths."*

The financial transactions that were brought together under the term banking had been taking place in one form or another for a long time previously and because of the central importance it has to the subject we are discussing, I think it would be useful at this point to take a brief look at how banking came into existence. Three main elements are involved each of which involves usury: foreign exchange, the negotiation of loans, and deposit banking, which includes the creation of money.

Merchants had been conducting international trade for many centuries and gradually a way of paying for goods abroad, without the necessity of having to carry great quantities of gold and silver around the world, was devised. The way it was done was by means of what were known as bills of exchange. In its simplest form this was a letter given by the buyer of the goods to the seller authorising an agent of the buyer in the home country of the seller to pay for the goods he had bought, so that the seller could collect the money he was owed in his own country and his own currency. These bills were always post-dated to allow time for the goods to be sold and the money transferred, and what began to happen was that merchants, who wanted to get hold of their money quickly, would sell the bill to another merchant who had ready cash, at less than its face value. This second merchant would then cash the bill in when it reached its due date and make a nice profit without having had to do anything at all. This was called discounting. Dealing in these bills became a more and more sophisticated business and before long there were merchants who found it more profitable to trade in bills than actual commodities. Their trade was pure usury. This was one of the transactions taken over by the banker.

The second element was the negotiation of loans. When a loan was made there would be the lender, usually a merchant with surplus capital, the borrower, frequently a landowner in need of ready cash and also a third party, a scrivener, mentioned in the quotation from Clarendon earlier. The scriveners or scribes were a professional group who had a monopoly in the writing of legal contracts and were therefore an indispensable part of the loan process. Being in the middle of the transaction they were in an ideal position to know both those who had money to lend and also those who were looking to borrow money. Gradually they began to take on an active role and instead of just writing down the contract they would set up the whole transaction charging a sizeable fee for doing so. From there to the final stage was but a short step. Rather than bringing together the two parties the scrivener would take the lender's money, agreeing to pay him a certain amount of interest and then lend it to the borrower at a higher rate of interest, pocketing the difference, thus exactly mirroring the main transaction of modern banking. In this way they were able to accommodate very large loans by taking from several lenders and passing on to one borrower. This transaction was also taken over by the banker.

The third element was deposit banking and this did mainly involve the goldsmiths. Because of the nature of their trade in precious metals and bullion, goldsmiths usually had secure strong-rooms and for centuries people had handed over to them their excess gold and silver and other valuables for safe-keeping, receiving in return a receipt for what they had deposited. After a time some people started to use these receipts instead of the gold itself, transferring the receipt to someone else's name when paying a large debt. Another thing people would do was write to the goldsmith authorising him to pay the bearer of the letter a certain amount from what they had on deposit, prefiguring the modern cheque. The goldsmith would make a charge for storage and for any services of this kind he performed. In this way, privately-issued notes did begin to make their appearance as a medium of exchange, but they were still tied to existing coinage and their total volume was very small in comparison with cash transactions that took place.

After a while, however, the goldsmiths realised that the deposits they held on behalf of other people tended to remain at a more or less constant level and they started to issue receipts over and above those they had already given out, both to pay for things for themselves and increasingly, as circumstances permitted, as loans at interest. The import ant thing to realise is that this new paper was entirely fictitious and not backed-up by currency at all. Money had been conjured out of thin air. This transaction which was not only usurious but quite frankly fraudulent, also became an integral part of the new banking.

Thus these three transactions, which were all originally connected to real trade, were gathered together in their usurious form under the umbrella term banking and entirely divorced from their original context. A new business was created dealing only in money itself. The vultures released by Calvin had well and truly come home to roost.

We left Cromwell fighting the Dutch. He won, of course, as he almost always did in battle. Had he been as successful a politician as he was general the history of England might have been considerably different but as it was, people were heartily glad to see the back of him, and were only too happy to welcome back the son of the executed king who returned to the throne of England as Charles II.

This event was bogusly known as the Restoration, bogusly because nothing was in fact restored. The situation had in fact completely changed. True, there was a king again, but in name only. He was now in no sense a ruler, merely a figurehead. Executive control was now firmly in the hands of Parliament and real power increasingly wielded by mercantile interests and the financiers who funded them. One of the conditions imposed by Parliament on the King was that he had to give up the ancient feudal dues in which the real power of the monarchy had rested in return for what was basically an income collected from revenue. Charles II was in effect a salaried employee of Parliament. His political impotence was reflected by his frivolous lifestyle and the negation of his covert attempts to restore the power of the monarchy.

When his brother James, who mounted the throne after him, made a more determined attempt to restore the old order, Parliament's speedy response was to invite William, Prince of Orange, who had married James's daughter, Mary, over from Holland to take over the throne. The terms on which he was to come were dictated by Parliament and by these terms any vestige of political power left with the monarchy was removed. William was quite literally the bankers' man. He brought with him a personal banker from Amsterdam and in his wake came many other financiers from that city, which was at that time the financial centre of Europe. From this time, however, Amsterdam went into decline and London became the new centre of world finance. This was the "Glorious Revolution".

The reign of William left basically three things to posterity. The first was the troubles in Ireland of which still we have bloody reminders every week which passes. The second was the Religious Toleration Act which in fact ensured once and for all that the state could no longer be bound by any religious restraints, since now all religious points of view were equally valid under the law. With the definitive removal of direct religious influence on government, the idea of the "rule of right" which had always been at least implicit was "replaced by economic expediency as the arbiter of policy and the criterion of political conduct." By this act any lingering religiously-based obstacles which still stood in the way of the financiers were removed. The third thing following on from this and enshrining the final triumph of the money-lenders was the foundation of the Bank of England. The usurers had won the day. The new Bank had government permission to discount bills and print as much money as it wanted. To cap it all, the National Debt was established. The Government secured from the Bank a large source of spending power in return for the promise to pay interest on a long-term basis. A specific portion of tax revenues was allocated to pay the interest. In other words, from now on the whole population were perpetually in debt. The money-lenders' wildest dreams had come true. From then on usurious transactions proceeded to adopt a larger and larger role in economic affairs until now they have so permeated everyday existence that life without them seems almost inconceivable. As a local bank manager said recently, in all seriousness, "Interest makes the world go round".

In presenting this historical overview, it has clearly been impossible for me to cover in detail the two hundred or so years involved and I have necessarily taken a particular thread and followed it through weft and warp of the historical continuum. However, when all the details are filled in, the conclusions that I have drawn will be seen to remain true and valid. My purpose was to show how, in a period of under two centuries, the transaction of usury changed from being a crime absolutely condemned since ancient times, subject to the severest penalties of the law and despised by all people, to being respected and recognised business practice whose practitioners were honoured with the highest possible accolades the state could award.

The rightness of the position of our earlier ancestors on this issue is made daily more clear as the insidious effects of usury make themselves more and more felt on the environment and in our lives. It is hoped that this seminar will help to focus attention on the harmful and destructive nature of usury, which has now become so inextricably bound up with modern life, and awaken awareness of it as an important political issue. Our forbears demonstrated that life is possible without it and it may well be that a cure for the otherwise terminal sickness of the society in which we live lies in the return to the ancient prohibition of it which formed the starting point of this paper.

Abdalhaqq Bewley

The False Growth Cycle Inherent in the Credit-based Economy Together with some Historical Illustrations

MODERN ECONOMISTS are obsessed with the idea of 'growth' – credit growth, money growth, economic growth – the list goes on. But the questions we must ask are: Is this growth sustainable? Is the whole concept of economic growth based on credit valid? Has it ever worked in the past?

What I intend to do in this talk is to illustrate an historical cycle which occurred in the major financial centres which were based on, or extensively relied on, "paper" money. In other words, they relied on credit. I will concentrate on certain European economies and focus on the pattern running from Genoa to Amsterdam to London to New York. To illustrate two different types of economy which fall outside of this pattern, I will refer to Venice of the 15th century and the Ottoman Empire prior to 1800 to illustrate prosperity without the extensive use of credit.

This talk will concentrate on "currency", for as Lord Keynes pointed out:

"There is no subtler or surer means of overturning the existing basis of society than to debauch the currency."
So the nature of currency is crucial.

Now, before leaping off into history, I will first touch on money and its function, and explain some of the transactions which we will refer to in the course of this talk.

The function of money is to separate buying from selling and thus enable people to trade without needing to have recourse to direct barter – like trading goats for wheat and the like. Money is therefore a medium of exchange, and by extension, it is also a unit of account so people can keep track of what they have more easily. Many things have been used as money in the course of history – salt, tobacco, pepper, cowry shells, etc., but gold and silver have been recognised and accepted as money for the past 2000 years. Gold and silver form a currency which owes its value to an inherent desirability. Both are worth something in themselves as commodities.

There are two types of paper "currency":

1. What can be termed as "fiduciary" money or promissory money, which bears the promise that it can be exchanged for gold or silver. So, in principle, it represents something of value.

2. Fiat money, which is issued by governments or banks and which is intrinsically worthless – bits of paper with no actual value in themselves other than the illusion of value. This is the form of currency in use today.

Since, as we have heard in the last talk, usury was absolutely forbidden by the church and those who were known to practise it forbidden communion in the church and sometimes even Christian burial, various credit devices were contrived to get around the prohibition and also to circumvent the need to move large sums of cash around. These devices were employed by the money dealers and lenders of the time. These transactions also enabled them to make themselves a handsome profit. Debt at that time was substantial. For example, in 1642, the total income of the 121 English peers was about 730,000 pounds – but their debts were 1,500,000. People were desperate to get hold of money by any means, and money lenders equally eager to make a profit off people's needs.

The major unit of credit they devised was THE BILL OF EXCHANGE.

The bill of exchange was a binding promise to pay a specific person a certain sum at some future but proximate date in another town, and hence a change into another currency. This in itself involved a loan, for even if a bill was payable "on sight", it still took time to be carried from one place to another before it could be paid. It was also agreed that for large sums the person required to pay should have time to raise that sum. This delay, known as USANCE, might be 1, 2 or 3 months from the day the bill was presented – so the merchant had a credit advance of 1 to 3 months. Fair enough, but the lenders had fixed rates of usance, or interest as we would call it today, – and also got additional profit on the loan by playing the exchange market. Some merchants would even send bills to themselves to gain credit, bills secured by absolutely no cash at all!

This transaction usually involved four people. Merchant A (call him Antonio of Genoa) owes money to Merchant B in Antwerp (call him Hans). Antonio needs to pay money to Hans, but does not know anyone in Antwerp who can pay Hans. So Antonio goes to a local banker, say the Casa di San Giorgio, which has an account with people in Antwerp, the Welsers. Antonio pays his money to the Casa which gives him a bill which he then sends to the Welsers. The Welsers then pay out the sum to Hans. Antonio has to pay the Casa more than he owed Hans to cover their interest. The difference between the two sums amounts to, say, a certain extra number of florins which is concealed interest.

These bills were also subject to discounting. Hans has this bill of exchange, but he doesn't actually have the money because the Welsers have a month in which to pay it to him. He goes to a discounter and says, "I have a bill of exchange for 300 florins at one month usance." The discounter buys it from him for 270 florins, so he has paid an interest of 10% a month to obtain this sum of money. It was clearly usury and definitely detested by the moralists of the time who saw through it.

Since the time of the Reformation, usury had become far easier in Protestant countries, and loans were effected by a simple promissory note stating to repay a certain sum at a certain date. These promissory notes could be assigned to creditors to pay another debt. Hans has a promissory note for 20 florins from Wilhelm. He owes Antonio 18 florins, so he gives him the note and signs it over to him. So it becomes a currency. Bills of exchange were also transferred. We also find goldsmiths and silversmiths handing out credit notes based on metal deposited with them and which then were passed from hand to hand as currency.

This is the origin of paper currency, used originally to conceal the usury involved.

Now we can move to our historical illustrations:

Genoa moved discreetly to the forefront of finance in the 1550's and the age of the Genoese lasted until 1627. I am missing out Antwerp, a hot bed of usury under the Fuggers and Welsers, because the use of paper really came into prominence in Genoa. The Fuggers complained that doing business with the Genoese meant playing with pieces of paper (*mit papier*) while they operated with real money (*Baargeld*). Genoa had to focus on paper in order to avoid the Canon laws on usury.

The focus of activity in Genoa centred on a group of banker-financiers (your early multinationals) who formed a joint bank, the Casa di San Giorgio, in 1408. By the 1530's the total debt handled by the Casa was 40 million lire (8 million ducats) which was divided into paper credit notes each worth 100 lire (20 ducats). In 1557, the Genoese took on the lucrative job of managing and moving Charles V's money for him. They lent him money at what they said was 10% – expenses, but 30% according to the royal secretaries. Profits were enormous – and, more importantly, their credit enabled them to control the silver bullion arriving from America. So they went one step further and then used the silver bullion to buy and control gold. As bills of exchange had to be paid in gold, the Genoese were given considerable power. When the King tried to sack them in 1575, they blocked the circulation of gold, the troops mutinied (and sacked Antwerp) and the king gave in. The whole system of commerce functioned through these bills of exchange, which they ultimately controlled.

Eventually it became too burdensome for them, – they could not keep up with the constant demands of Spain and after the Spanish bankruptcy of 1627 they more or less withdrew. It was getting out of hand as they were lending more capital than they had, at a low return and they had the good Italian sense to recognise that. So Genoa was the first to develop the paper system of bills as a mechanism to monopolize credit and to make usury not so apparent. They bequeathed this paper system to the rest of Europe.

Amsterdam, the centre of 17th century financial activity, had been growing steadily all the time, gradually displacing Genoa. It was aided by the flocks of refugees who came there, particularly the Sephardic Jews who were the masters of currency and stock exchange at that time.

Initially, Amsterdam began as a commodity centre, the usual starting point for most financial centres. It collected, stored, sold and resold all manner of goods and had a virtual monopoly on transport. Accounts were settled by transfers using fictional "bank money" with interest of 5%, so the Dutch rarely had recourse to coin. The banks' bookkeepers would deal with 10 or 12 million florins a day on paper.

The credit market was handled by firms and merchants. But gradually, as was the case with Genoa, the commodity trade declined and they became more and more a credit market for lenders and borrowers than a commodity market for buyers and sellers. The goods bypassed Amsterdam and the Dutch became "the bankers of Europe".

The use of bills of exchange grew and they were used in lieu of cash. They were preferred because they bore interest (through discounting and underwriting).

The flood of paper grew – to 4, 5, 10 or 15 times the amount of real money in circulation. Sometimes it consisted of chains of unsecured bills (*wisselruiterij*) based on promises without any collateral at all. All the paper converged on Amsterdam, leaving it only to return to it again. So the basic mechanism of the commercial system was provided by the crisscross movements of bills of exchange.

There was always a great deal of specie cash under it all, just as there had been in Genoa. Vast sums of gold and silver flowed into Amsterdam but it was the reputation of Amsterdam that allowed risky deals of chains of paper, secured only by the prosperous reputation of the Dutch economy.

The power of the money men of Amsterdam was such that they could put 200 million florins in paper money into circulation at the drop of a hat.

This very prosperity, based on paper, led to the usual embarrassing surplus so that Amsterdam had too much credit to invest. There weren't enough people to borrow this created credit, so the Dutch turned to modern states – notoriously good at consuming money, and bad at repaying it. Loans were made wildly – to the Hapsburg Emperor, the Elector of Saxony, the Elector of Bavaria, the King of Denmark, the King of Sweden, Catherine II of Russia, the King of France, the city of Hamburg (their rivals!) and the American rebels. Perhaps they had "loan quotas"! The over supply of money in Amsterdam is shown by the fact that it was being loaned at only 3%

or even 2% (exactly as happened in Genoa in 1600). There was too much credit on paper available.

To get an idea of the state that Dutch finances reached (or sank to), let us examine the figures for 1782. Total capital amounted to a thousand million florins. 900 million was invested in loans, and only 50 million or 5.5% of the total was in gold or silver. The rest was paper. Some people were living very dangerously indeed.

The inevitable crises arose, beginning in the 1760's. The first crisis followed the Seven Years' War (1756-63), which was a very prosperous time for Holland, as it had been neutral. This surge of prosperity exacerbated the situation, resulting in free-for-all extensions of bills of exchange and chains of unsecured paper. Credit piled up in a paper mountain 15 times that of cash. Discounters had to stop discounting and there was a currency shortage. Bankruptcies resulted – one firm went with debts of 6 million florins, another with debts of 1,200,000 florins. Bank money plummeted. The stock market came to a standstill.

The situation was only saved by a cash injection. Some people had installed factories for refining bad money issued by Frederick II of Prussia. Local merchants arranged to collect the coins and send them to merchants in Amsterdam via family connections. They, in turn, drew bills of exchange on the metal, enabling the big merchants to survive through an injection of real money.

There was yet another crisis in 1773 when an English firm went bankrupt with debts of 5 million florins. The same chain of events happened – the Stock Market stopped – other firms went down.

Those who had real money or goods survived. Those up to the necks in nothing but paper went down. But really, by this time, people were looking more and more towards England. What had happened in Genoa happened in Amsterdam. The creation of credit, unsupported by real money, generated enormous growth. Money had been created out of thin air, credit grew to unmanageable proportions, bad loans were made, and bankruptcies resulted. The situation proved to be intrinsically unstable.

When discussing currency and paper, it is, of course, impossible to avoid mentioning the notorious South Sea Bubble and the Great Crash that followed it. But first, I would like to cross over to my two other examples, Venice and Ottoman Turkey. I think we have a pretty good picture of the financial mechanisms of the Genoa-Amsterdam system and if we move over in more or less the same zone, it makes for a good comparison.

Early Venice was a model which was based on trade, and counters the argument that without extensive credit (manufactured out of nothing), there can be no prosperity nor a flourishing economy. I will concentrate on the 15th century, the real peak of Venetian trade.

Venice occupied a very advantageous geographical position – she controlled the Adriatic and the trade with Syria and Egypt. She had excellent contacts with Germany and Central Europe to whom she sold cotton, pepper and spice and who provided her with silver coins to use for purchases in the Levant. There was also a Venice-Bruges-London route.

She expanded into an Empire, occupying towns like Padua and

Verona, and became very wealthy indeed. The receipts of the Signoria alone, the city of Venice, for 1423, amounted to 750,000 gold ducats. Equivalent to a per capita income between 50 and 100 ducats. Very high indeed for the time. In England the yearly income for the lord of a good-sized manor was about 12 ducats.

This was all based on trade and a state of peace (unlike the financiers who thrive on war to create debt). Return on foreign trade at the time was 40%, – all based on major commodities – pepper, spices, Syrian cotton, grain, wine and salt.

Mind you, trade was only free for Venetians. Following the pattern they had experienced trading in the Middle East, they confined German merchants to a special residence. Germans had to deposit their goods there and sell them and buy Venetian goods under strict supervision. Venetian merchants were forbidden to buy and sell directly in Germany, so the Germans had to come to Venice with their goods, including silver, essential for trading with the Muslim lands.

The state also undertook to build large merchant ships for charter. There was an annual auction and the winner collected charters from other merchants and charged them for the freight, based on amount of goods. These "pools" were open to any Venetian merchant, but the authorities were quick to disband any cartel which seemed to be forming a monopoly.

Venice was much more conservative than other Italian states and, as you can see, a central feature was the strong control of the government, which itself was composed of merchants.

As for finances, usury was not the mainstream of economic life in Venice, unlike Genoa.

The primary commercial instrument was the commercial loan, the *colleganza*, and 90% of the time this involved a partnership deal. A merchant would provide all the capital and then get his capital back plus ¼ of the profits, or he would put up ¼ of the capital and get back his capital plus 50% of the profits. The entire populace supplied credit for the voyages and the whole system was self-contained and self-sustained. Merchants worked on a deal-to-deal basis. Accounts had to be settled within 30 days of a ship's return. The bill of exchange was never more than that – limited to the duration of its journey. Venice was content with its own ways and not interested in financing others. Commodity trade was the life blood of Venice, not finance.

When Venice declined in the 16th century, the major factor was external – the fall of Constantinople to the Turks. Venetians and Turks fought each other off and on for 250 years, and prosperity drained away.

This brings us to the Ottoman Empire, which was a strong and vigorous state in its heyday. It was full of large, populous trading cities. The grass roots level of the economy was what is described as the "bazaar economy", that is, a market economy centred around the cities and regional fairs where exchange followed traditional rules and was characterized by good faith.

In 1550 (when Genoa was on the rise), everything in Turkey was exchanged for cash – no papers, no loan-sheets or ledgers – and no credit transactions involving interest. Even under the influence of western merchants, this old way was slow to change. We have the occasional bill of exchange (*suftaja*), but its function was just that. A western merchant could transfer his excess balance from Constantinople to his agent in Aleppo without interest. There were no banks, or speculative transactions. What we do find are partnerships, Venetian style arrangements and credit without interest.

What we notice about commercial life there was the low prices of everything compared to western Europe. The further away you get from financial centres, the lower the prices. There weren't a lot of actual coins in circulation, but that didn't affect normal commercial life. The backbone of Turkish independence lay in the caravans which were strictly controlled by the state, thereby giving her control over her trade and resources. Most of her seas were protected as well. Furthermore, Ottoman merchants thwarted penetration by foreign merchants who were allocated their own quarters in the cities and kept under surveillance.

The decline in the Turkish Empire started around 1800 in the Balkans due to European influence. The advance of the European system proved destructive, the state lost authority, foreign goods flooded the market thereby destroying native industry, and the economy became sluggish. War also put a strain on the economy – especially the constant conflict with Russia.

So we see from these two instances that prosperity is possible without usury. A paper-based system is not the only alternative.

But to return to our theme of usurious growth, let's look at the notorious South Sea Bubble, which ensnared many people into the use of paper. The South Sea Bubble is, in effect, an accurate although dramatic manifestation of the cycle of reliance on paper money – sixty years of artificial growth compressed into 6 months.

Following the various wars with Holland, England had built up a rather large debt. In 1694, the Bank of England was established to help fund William of Orange in fighting France, and was described by its founder, William Paterson, as designed to "*have the benefit of the interest of all money which it creates out of nothing*". This is a clear articulation of the unreality of paper money. Then something had to be done about the debts generated by the government through the Bank. In 1711, all holders of government short-term obligations (some 9 million pounds) became shareholders, whether they liked it or not, in the "South Sea Company". This was designed to amalgamate England's floating debt into a single unified sum like the advertisements you see in the press to take one big loan to pay off all your debts. However, in this case, rather than being a loan, it was shares in a company. So while England's credit was good, her debts were enormous.

Short-term and long-term commitments (some secured on tax revenues for the next 80 years) amounted to 40 million pounds. All were at 6% interest, so the government had to find over 2,500,000 million pounds every year to pay its creditors, which was a vast sum in those days. The government was therefore on the lookout for ways of dealing with this debt.

They looked to France which was also deeply in debt and saw

something quite interesting. A Scot, John Law, had been given free rein to establish a system which included the formation of an overseas trading company, popularly known as the Mississippi Company. This was infamously known as Law's Experiment. He accepted government securities as payment for shares in the company. In other words, people exchanged the debts the government owed them for shares in the company. Because the company was backed by the government, the value of the shares increased dramatically – the price of a 500 livre share went up to 18,000 livres.

When the English government saw this, it thought it would be a jolly good way of reducing its debt, and so it decided to use the South Sea Company in the same way as Law had used the Mississippi company. Government creditors were able to exchange their bonds for shares in the South Sea Company – for a sum – and get the dividends, if there were any. Within a year, 80% of these debts were converted into shares. The price went from 120 to 950 in six months.

Then things got out of hand. When the French Mississippi company was only able to bring in a 2% dividend, people's confidence in the South Sea Company plummeted. People sold and sold, and the Great Crash began. South Sea stock went from 775 points to 520 to 170 in 6 weeks. Anxiety led people to hold on to hard cash and coins disappeared from circulation and could only be borrowed at 5% per month. In Ireland, commerce was practically reduced to direct barter. The government had got rid of some of its debt and got more people used to dealing in paper, people who would have had absolutely nothing to do with paper before this time. It was somewhat like convincing people to buy shares in British Telecom or

BP in order to make them more at ease with a new type of financial transaction. More people began to think about making more from bits of paper. What we see here is a miniature of the whole bubble credit cycle which shows that unreal growth is entirely dependent on people's faith in it and once belief in it goes, there is an inevitable collapse.

Eventually, in 1816, England ended up on the gold standard, but by this point England was already using paper issued by banks. Gold and silver were only lesser currencies. The war with France required the export of specie (cash) to the Continent to finance the war, so Pitt persuaded Parliament to pass the Bank Restriction Act. It laid down the compulsory exchange rate for notes and made them "temporarily" non-convertible. This remained in force for 24 years. The bank notes – with no guarantee behind them – circulated without losing any value in relation to metal. A French man living in England during the Napoleonic Wars said that he had never seen a single gold guinea the whole time he was there.

So the real guarantee for the paper was now neither gold nor silver, but the output and prosperity of Britain. And the size of the national debt was substantial – it went from 30 million pounds in 1748 to 834 million pounds in 1815. Even so, the popular press still showed unease at the use of paper money. The common people were scathing about the whole process, especially in view of the fact that by this time it was child's play to manipulate the money market if you had the clout. For example, when the Rothschilds were excluded from the loans floated by the Barings to help finance the war with Napoleon, they bought up shares, beared the market, and forced the various governments and the Barings to back down and bring them in. Nathan Rothschild was able to force the Bank of England to discount his own personal bills by paralysing the Bank by redeeming vast quantities of their notes for gold – 210,000 pounds in one day. Great power was now vested in the credit brokers, and it still made people uneasy.

The Bank of England tried to control the issuing of paper money by smaller banks to ensure their own monopoly. But on the other side of the Atlantic, the American colonies found it far easier to use promissory notes as money and Benjamin Franklin (who owned the press which printed the money) was a great advocate of this idea. In the middle of the 18th century, Parliament forbade the colonies to issue paper money and this was a cause of great resentment in America. Masses of notes called "Continentals" were printed in the Revolution and soon they were worth nothing. The expression, "Not worth a Continental" became famous at this time, meaning something utterly worthless. But what it did demonstrate was that certain people no longer had any qualms about putting something into circulation that was worth absolutely nothing.

The history of money has its own special chapter in the United States for the general credit trend encountered a hiccup there. There was always a certain animosity to banks, and debt, in certain quarters. Thomas Jefferson said that "banks are to be feared more than standing armies" and he stated that no nation had the right to contract debts not payable within the lifetime of the contractors, fixing 19 years as the limit of validity of such debts. There was a bitter conflict between the sound money men and those who loved to print paper to make credit boom. Andrew Jackson brought down the Bank of the United States in the 1830's by blocking the renewal of its charter, seeking a return to gold and silver and sound money. There was a determined shift away from paper towards gold and silver on the part of the people. This is the only instance where there was such a reversal of the general trend and is worth looking into.

Meanwhile in England, the shift from commerce to financial income was well under way. In 1870, Britain had a third of world trade, by 1914 it only had a seventh. Overseas investments doubled in order to use up the credit which was too massive to be used up at home. The familiar pattern was under way. World War I basically finished off Britain, leaving her with debts on which the annual interest was 326 MILLION POUNDS. The carrier of the credit/ growth monster moved across the Atlantic. Genoa – Amsterdam – London – New York. The bubble of prosperity, overstretching itself each time while growing bigger each time, moves on to batten itself on the resources of another location.

By 1930, the USA was the world's principal creditor. Mind you, at the time, the USA was sucking Europe dry by demanding the repayment of war debts which only came to an end in December 1933 (Hoover moratorium). Gold flowed into the USA, although by that time the USA and Great Britain had both gone off the gold standard. Beyond this point, we move into the massive debts generated by World War II, and we move into the arena of Bretton Woods and the IMF and paper currencies balanced against each other in terms of fictional money, with New York as the main financial centre.

There are several things that we notice in this cycle. First there is the growth of commodity trade. This upsurge in prosperity brings in the money men, the credit brokers who can make money from money without trading in real goods. At this point, paper and transactions in money without goods come into play to maximise profits for the credit broker.

This system is not in the best interests of the people and this is recognised by the financiers themselves. There is a letter from the Rothschild Bros. to the firm of Ikieheimer, Morton and Van Der Gould (25th Jan. 1863) in which John Sherman (future secretary of the Treasury of the USA) is quoted as saying:

"Those few who can understand the system will be busy getting profits while the general public will probably never suspect that the system is absolutely against their interests."

This system frequently generates deficit spending, which is financed by creating money and offering credit. This creates a great balloon of prosperity which far outstrips the real wealth in the system. It also generates inflation and creates a system which is intrinsically unstable. All this credit must go looking for someone who wants to borrow and this inevitably involves lending money to bad risks – insolvent governments – who default eventually because they cannot keep up with the interest payments which they must find from REAL resources or borrow more to pay off the interest on the credit. Does this sound familiar?

On the other hand, the system in which we saw real prosperity and growth were based on trade in commodities, rather than on making money out of money and creating money out of nothing. In those societies, partnerships with shared risk proved to be an effective way of obtaining credit. Also we note that the governments in these systems had strong controls over what went on in their markets. They were not, by any means, laissez-faire. Indeed, the Ottomans even had inspectors who went through the markets three times a week and severe penalties were imposed on anyone found to be illegally conducting business, including public humiliation. There must be some deterrent to prevent people from yielding to the temptation of getting something for nothing.

To conclude, in the usurocratic system, to use Ezra Pound's delightful term, the bubble of prosperity, although enticing, is not real and eventually stretches itself to the point where there is nothing tangible to back it up – as we saw in Genoa, Amsterdam and so on. The whole system must eventually break down because it is not based on anything real and the illusory prosperity will eventually be totally unsustainable. As we have seen historically, growth based on empty credit is fragile and intrinsically unstable.

Aisha Bewley

Usury-free and Usurious Economies Compared

To FURTHER describe and define the nature of an economy using the technique of usury, we can compare characteristics of three types of economy:

– A tribal economy

– The free market or credit economy of today

– An economy with a bimetallic currency without usury

But first, what IS this activity that we call economy? It is almost impossible to see it, overlaid as it is with the effects and techniques of interest bearing credit, where the means of exchange – money – has also become a trade in itself.

Economic activity might be simply described as mutually beneficial exchange, the ways in which man provides for his material well-being. How this is done can determine social stability or lack of it. The activity does reduce down to human behaviour. How a person makes an exchange or does business is based on their character. Economics has a social setting and is about social behaviour and political relationship.

A view of other types of economy can make this clear. It can indicate what sort of parameters define an economic system and what is desirable and what is not. What a balanced economic system might be like. We can begin to define parameters of what might constitute a mutually beneficial exchange. So, we will start by looking at a tribal economy. Please note that these definitions are necessarily generalised as most economies of a particular type will contain some elements of other types.

A tribal economy was in a relative sense a closed system, limited geographically, technically and culturally. Exchanges of goods or wealth were intrinsically part of social relations, confirming kinship and client/patron ties in a hierarchy of family, clan and tribe. The Tuareg nomads (before the introduction of a cash based economy by the French), would rarely sell their main source of wealth, livestock, except in extreme situations. They might be given as dowries or gifts or they might be lent to help kinsmen build up herds decimated by drought or disease, or given as blood-money to solve legal disputes. Social standing and sometimes economic survival were the rewards of these exchanges.

The behavioural nature of the exchanges were important. Men were praised for their generosity, fair dealing and hospitality. The system was communal and local and ethnically circumscribed. Exchange activity was further limited by the nature of productive activity. There was little specialisation and every household expected to provide for itself the essentials of food, shelter and clothing. Craft-based production required the simplest technology.

It was a subsistence type of economy, any surplus being by the grace of sufficient rainfall. Production was under natural constraints which were accepted and catered for in economic, social and political strategies, for example, seasonal moving of livestock to another region. It was not an economy that required continuous growth and it remained generally in balance with its environment. There were checks built into the social and political system to avoid over exploitation of the environment, for example, the allotment of specific grazing areas to tribal groups and clans.

So in general you have an economy limited in the actual amount and variety of exchange, that exchange being tied into social transactions, limited in geographical extent, economically constrained and controlled by environmental, social and political elements and lacking in a generalised means of exchange to extend the flexibility of barter. Usury was not generally a part of this type of economy.

When a cash currency or even barter goods are introduced from outside, the result has always been the destruction of the political and social organisation of that society, a disruption of their strategies for survival. For example, this has been a major element in the settlement and absorption of nomadic peoples, or the destruction of their fragile balance with the ecosystem in which they live. The introduction of a cash system had the effect of detaching exchange transactions from a strictly social dimension to become one about exchange for consumption. It gave transactions a range beyond that of the tribe, breaking its restrictively local character and introducing economic, social and political elements that were foreign to it.

Diametrically opposed to this tribal economy is the 'free market' economy of today. The definitions of it given here are widely accepted amongst economists as classical definitions. The free market economy developed out of the medieval economy which itself had many characteristics similar to the tribal. A prerequisite of economic life in the market system, is that exchange transactions become detached from the social and religious spheres of life, to emerge into a special category of their own. This then allows, and the system requires it, the total monetisation of all economic activity. Every task must have a monetary reward, and all must be involved in buying and selling. To quote an economist "the emergence of a separate economic sphere of activity visible within, and separate from, the surrounding matrix of social life". An example from the early days of this economy would be the monetisation of feudal dues. What had been given in kind or labour eventually had to be given as cash. Or today one can give many extreme examples where this process – the desire to put a price on everything – has reached its extremes and is part of the complete break up of our 'social fabric'. Residential homes for grandmother and grandfather and paid social workers are two examples.

Secondly, the stable and relatively unchanging state of the tribal economy contrasts with the idea of an expanding economy, a growing scale of production. In a system that has no economic responsibility towards men beyond the payment of the price asked – that price of labour or goods becomes a critical matter – the desire to get the best price became a necessity. Ideas of profit, of change, of social mobility, reflected the results of this monetisation of society. Mercantile interests were imbued with ideas of growth from the new results of international trade and moneylending.

Again the classical description of the free market economy defines three basic constituents of the productive process, calling them 'factors of production'. These are labour, land and capital. The elements of production analytically defined and so changed to a form to be quantified, to be given a price. These do not exist as eternal categories of social organisation. They might be seen as categories of nature: the soil, human effort, and the artifacts that can be applied to production but they do not naturally have the specific separation that distinguishes them in a market society. Land, labour, and capital are inextricably mixed and mingled in political and social relations in the pre-market society. How did these categories become distinct? All of them can be seen in the form required by the free market to be creations of usury. Free, wage earning, contractual labour ceased to be a part of an explicitly social relationship, and became a quantum of effort, a commodity to be disposed of in the market place for the best price it could bring, quite devoid of any reciprocal responsibilities on the part of the buyer beyond the payment of wages. As we have seen in our historical view, this labour was that of the peasant or copyholder, dispossessed of his land. As we have seen, moneylending was a major factor in these dispossessions.

A slight aside – but I think it is pertinent: This is no different from what is happening often in the Third World today. Credit and debt are the trap and the smallholding ends up as part of the larger estate. It is no different from the repossessed house or the bankrupt farmer here. As long as we have this mechanism of usury, the usurer will have his pound of flesh.

Our second factor of production is land – rentable, profit producing land, that could be bought and leased for the economic return it could yield. This conception of freely disposable land having monetary value did not exist in the tribal or medieval economy where land was bound up in social and political ties and obligations.

In the free market it became a property with a market price. Dues and payments in kind gave way to a single return of rent. It followed that land had to be put to profitable use. This changed relationship to land and change of ownership is again related to the activities of moneylenders.

Our third factor of production is capital. With the monetisation and commercialisation of society, property becomes expressible in monetary terms. Property was previously a sum of tangible wealth, a hoard, a treasury of plate bullion or jewels. A man now became worth so many pounds. Property became capital manifesting itself no longer in specific goods but as an abstract sum of infinitely flexible use whose value was its capacity to earn interest or profits. A transformation in thought from real wealth to abstract valuation, to calculation, to usury. The monetisation of exchanges in the society and their consequent and necessary detachment from social settings resulted in major changes in the nature of social accountability in these transactions. No longer could obligation, custom, responsibility restrain men's behaviour toward each other.

The employer's obligation to the labourer went no further than the payment of his wages and the landowner's responsibility for land no further than producing a profit from it. In the theory of the free market, and it had to have a theory, as it was not a natural form of economy, a new form of social control over the market had to be posited that would take over from the traditional forms.

Here it was seen as a pattern of social behaviour that the environment of the free market itself imposed on society. Note here this reversal in control. What was this pattern of behaviour? It was the drive to maximise one's income by concluding the best possible bargains in the market place. This was obviously not new in human terms but the system made it necessary. For example, when the peasant farmer sold a few eggs in the local market in the pre-market economy, these were not necessarily critical to his existence. However, with the monetisation of labour, the profit-seeking market-transactions became predominant. Now everything was for sale, and the terms of the transactions were anything but subsidiary to existence. To a man who sold his labour in the market in a society that assumed no responsibility for his upkeep, the price at which he concluded his bargain was all important. And so it was with the landlord and the budding capitalist. Men were not free to follow their self interest – they were forced to follow it. As Robert L. Heilbroner said "Thus a pattern of economic maximization was generalised throughout society and given an inherent urgency that made it a powerful force for shaping human behaviour." The market mechanism was self-interest.

And how does a socially workable arrangement emerge from such a socially dangerous set of motivations? Adam Smith, the philosopher of the free market, says 'Competition' will control and adjust any unfair or excessive prices, wage rates and production quantities. So justice and correct social behaviour became dependent on competition. From motivations of self-interest, of maximisation of returns in the market place, it is a natural step to require increase, to require growth.

Growth was needed to supply the beginnings of a mass consumer market – to supply those who had been uprooted from their self-sufficient existences. Growth in economic terms is an increase in the output of goods for exchange. The technique of the division of labour or specialisation, with the needed application of large amounts of capital, borrowed at interest, financing the jump in scale from a home-based craft operation to a factory operation, was the essence of the production process of the free market. Growth was sustained by ever finer divisions of labour and ever greater injections of capital to finance new machinery and techniques.

The nature and scale of this industrial production make social control and accountability difficult. Decisions affecting a community and its environment are made remote from it. Adam Smith theorised that such problems would be taken care of by natural market forces. That perhaps held good when the economy was made up of many small independent producers but did not take into account the consequences of the kind of growth that occurred when credit was freely available and continually expanding. Production became mass-production and the scale of operations resulted in competition becoming a destructive rather than a balancing force. Production became increasingly concentrated in the hands of relatively few. This resulted in price-setting and so ended the role of price competition and the theoretical restraints imposed by the consumer in the free market. In the modern version of the free market, business, labour and government have maintained a charade of this so-called consumer sovereignty (what people want) but their remoteness, sheer size and bureaucratic organisation make it difficult to bring them to account.

The requirement of finance for production, in the form of credit, has become a necessary fact of life, due to the scale of production and to the control of the form of the debt economy. But it has an echo, an echo down history, of the craftsman being indebted to his supplier of raw materials. What was usually the condition of things in the bad times became permanent. The lender got power over the borrower by credit, and the situation became permanent.

Money has become credit. How did this occur? In the free market, where everything is given a cash value, money becomes of central importance.

The devaluation of money itself from a precious metal commodity to paper, to electronic impulses, is the creation of the moneylender. Much of it is usury. And all of it had its origin in usury – the transformation of the gold into the promissory-note, handed on as currency itself. This paper allowed the vast expansion of credit. The Exchanges internationally and the banks nationally were the means by which the credit was distributed. Their main business began as and still is the giving of loans with interest. Eventually, through the formation of central banks, the medium became a means of controlling the whole direction of the economy through manipulating the supply of money and the restriction or expansion of credit.

The free market saw the evolution of money from being a passive means of exchange based on precious metals to being a mechanism of control over the economy as a whole. Banking and modern monetary methods and theory are described in books as economics. They are not economics, they are something fastened onto economy.

They are in fact usury.

Economy of Natural Balance

Between the two extremes of the tribal and the free market economy there must be one of natural balance.

What elements would this 'naturally balanced economy' have? It would have elements such as: exchange taking place freely and yet there could be particular limits on exchange at just those points where we have seen it is necessary. These limits relate to justice and natural balance, and protect the stability of society by ensuring just behaviour between men in their economic exchanges.

It might also address the form and scale of economy so that exchanges are generally limited to transactions between individuals without anonymous technical or bureaucratic intermediaries. Particular concern would also be given to discourage transactions wherein one man can gain power over another in economic exchange.

Moderation of extremes such as an unbalanced distribution of wealth, and growth or contraction of an excessive kind would also feature in this economy.

This economy would not have a theory about how it works, as would be based on the natural system of simple exchange, hand to hand, that is universal.

Basic principles would be dislike of unnatural increase, of uncertainty in transactions, of delay and deferment in transactions, of the creation of debt, of speculation. It would allow for the protection of the integrity of the means of exchange, and make special stipulations about commerce in necessities such as food. The law would be defined in terms of exchanges that are permitted or not permitted.

It might be thought that this emphasis on the law would produce a situation hemmed in and constrained. This need not be the case in practice.

Because of the nature of what is allowed and what is not allowed it would result in money and goods moving rapidly through the market. Exchange would be immediate and simple, hand to hand, with no delay, money changing hands rapidly and accumulation and hoarding discouraged.

Transactions would be completed before the buyer and seller part, with agreement, and in general nothing left hanging over. There would be less debt. It would be the form of the simple market place, without restriction in its expansion out to international trade, when there is a currency with value and equivalence. The means of exchange would be gold and silver, with nothing representing them.

These metals have always been universally accepted as having value in themselves, and in this they are like goods for barter. In this economy cash would only be gold and silver. Equivalence between coinage and other forms of the metal would be protected by the law and there would be no profitable trade in currency itself. Keeping gold and silver out of circulation by hoarding would be forbidden.

The major prohibitions would centre round the question of unnatural increase, of usury, both on money and goods. For example when exchanging gold for gold (as in a currency exchange) or silver for silver, either by weight or by number of coins, it would be forbidden for there to be any element of increase at all in the exchange. This maintains the equivalence of different currencies, prevents trade in them, so gold would be free to travel anywhere. It ensures that there would be no unnatural increase that is made without effort, delayed payment (credit) and delayed delivery of goods, creating debts, being prohibited in many transactions, and in general disliked in others as they open the door to increase by usury. Both delayed payment and delayed delivery of goods together in an exchange would be forbidden, as this is selling a debt for a debt. Delayed payment and loans with increase would be forbidden in all transactions.

The effects of these prohibitions are easy to see. With no increase on loans or deferred payments, credit would only be given as a non-profit service. It would not happen so often and society would not be full of lenders and borrowers. Growth in trade and industry would be from internally generated capital rather than external injections – organic rather than artificial growth. Equality between men politically and socially in economic activity would be undisturbed and so society would retain its stability. The unnatural increase and growth required and caused by usury, the bringing of everything into its orbit and control, subservient to it, until it places institutions and techniques over economy, that look like economy and are called economy but are not: all this could not occur.

Other major prohibitions would centre round uncertainty in transactions. For example, it would be forbidden to sell fruit that has not begun to ripen on the tree. Stockpiling, cornering the market to raise prices, or undercutting in the market would all be forbidden. Exchange transactions involving food would be given special attention. For example, it would be forbidden to resell foodstuffs until you have physically taken possession of them.

As in the free market economy the factors of production, land, labour and capital are available, but the lack of credit financing, would prevent concentration of production into large scale units. This results in a spread across society of a large number of small independent producers, both in manufacturing and agriculture, a situation that would maintain to a degree both craft production and self-sufficient agriculture, and allow many more people in the society to be their own masters. Ventures involving capital would usually be partnerships of merchants brought together for that purpose and then dissolved again. The scale of capital would not be large.

So there you have the three economies. They are incomplete and simplified views but I think they give a taste of other possibilities.

The sort of limits put on economic activity that we have described, that protect social stability and make those engaged in transactions accountable, would virtually rule out all economic transactions that occur in our society today. Commodity trading, futures trading, currency trading, stock exchange speculation, bank financed development, hire purchase agreements, mortgages, unit trusts and so on and so on...

Abdalhalim Orr

The Setting

THE AIM of this part of the programme is to provide an answer to the question "What kind of society is it that not only permits but condones and actively encourages usury?" I believe that this is a question of central importance since our answer is in fact the point of this seminar – not the subject of it but certainly the point, because in the end it's not just a question of usury.

We have heard so far today about the real definition of usury and about the traditional attitudes towards it, from Plato and Aristotle in the classical tradition and from Judaeo-Christian sources in the Bible. We have noted the progression from St. Augustine at the beginning of the Dark Ages in the 4th century AD, to Thomas Aquinas in the Renaissance nearly 1000 years later, re-affirming Aristotle's judgement that usury is a barren form of money-making and as such is unnatural and so unjustifiable.

We have seen how attitudes began to change from the Reformation in the 16th century, through the English revolutions of the 17th, and the forging of modern banking practices, particularly in London, Genoa and Amsterdam by the 18th century.

We've been given a vivid picture of the seriousness of the current state of affairs in the world and the essentially negative contribution, not to say outright delinquency, of financial agencies at this critical time. We've seen how modern men and women have been persuaded – collectively and on a global scale – to make the great leap of imagination required to imbue with value inherently worthless fiat money – money that doesn't even represent real wealth – and this despite repeated disastrous crises of confidence with whole fortunes being wiped out practically overnight.

All of this makes me want to stop for a moment and wonder about the how and why of these things. And having considered where all this has come from, to imagine where it might all be leading.

The point for me is: "what is it about us, about modern people, about the modern world, which has allowed usury to become such a huge part of our lives?" Why was it so roundly condemned by 18th century moralists like Kant, who, towards the end of that century in 1795, spoke of "the ingenious system of international credit invented by a commercial people in this century which shows the power of money in its most dangerous form"?

I would like to show in this paper that the answer as to how and why usury has come to dominate economic affairs lies in what can and should be viewed as a general decline in morality and ethical behaviour. In order to do this I will give a brief sketch of two distinct, and in many ways, opposing world views:

– on metaphysics and the nature of reality.

– on the role and scope of human reason.

– on the basis of ethics.

Historically these two views began in practice to diverge significantly over just this period we have been looking at, from the Renaissance, through the Reformation, early modern times and the Enlightenment to the Victorians and to date. Over this period one widely accepted worldview has been supplanted by another; though I should emphasise that I am not suggesting a 'good old days' scenario, at least as far as Europe is concerned. By worldview or '*weltanschauung*' I mean the inner landscape, the whole world of meanings which we inhabit as human beings. We might even go so far as to say that in the last 500 years or so human beings' understanding of themselves and their world – at least in the West, and of course our Western worldview is rapidly predominating across the world in this century – has changed more radically and fundamentally than at any other period in history. I find this significant – so what I'm going to do then is to outline these two ways of looking at the world and to show that usury is but one, albeit an important, facet of what amounts to a moral issue, in fact *the* moral issue, since we will be talking about the principle of 'right and wrong', or 'good and bad' and not any particular instance of moral or immoral behaviour such as honesty or lying, charity or theft, philanthropy or usury.

In order to give even this outline sketch, I hope you forgive me if we have to go a little slowly because I want to make sure that the issues at stake are quite clear. I will describe in philosophical, social and psychological terms those aspects of our modern society forming the context in which usury has found such fertile soil.

The first overall philosophical position, or worldview, holds as a basic and fundamental principle that not all realities have a material existence: that an abstract or 'intelligible' world, to use Kant's term, has its own transcendental or metaphysical reality beyond and distinct from the material or 'sensible' world of time and space that constitutes the immediate facts of our workaday experience. It is not easy to speak succinctly about this distinction between abstract and concrete, but a few examples will clarify things and I'm sure you all know what I'm getting at, although there are curious implications in this potentially, though not inevitably, dualist doctrine.

This Platonist conception of abstract entities is perhaps best illustrated by numbers. Certainly it seems clear that a number has no material form – how many twos are there in this room? Show me three-ness – what is the ten-ness of, for example, your fingers? The talk of discovering rather than inventing new and ever greater prime numbers clearly seems to indicate that they are somewhere 'out there', independent of our cognition of them, waiting in the wings, so to speak.

Consider also the game of chess, for example. What is chess exactly? The sum total of all boards, pieces and moves? This would be a taxonomic view – identification by labelling. Or is chess essentially the rules by which the game is played? And if so, what is the ontological reality of these rules? That is, in what do these rules have their being? Not their existence, since that term is properly restricted to material facts, but their being – where are the rules of chess or any other game or rule-governed activity for that matter? Now what about such qualities as beauty, truth and justice? We do seem to be able to recognise and respond to these things in some innate way, but what are they?, and where do they come from?

Here there are, in fact, two answers. The first, which corresponds to the view I have been discussing, is that their reality is abstract just as numbers are abstract and just as, I will argue, the moral imperative, the truly moral impulse to do good for its own sake, must be abstract in that it IS, it has its being or reality, prior to any context in which we might identity its working. We need a name for this view, so for the sake of convenience I will call it the 'Right View'.

The other view holds that everything is material, exists as matter in time and space, and is governed by the 'laws' of motion and other physical laws conditioning the behaviour of particles, elements, compounds and so on, so that number, truth, beauty, justice and the rest exist only in our cognition of them, which is to say, exist simply as electrochemical impulses in our brains, for which we are biologically pre-programmed.

This view is certainly not modern, it was known to the ancient Greeks who called it atomism and it doesn't seem to have been taken particularly seriously by most people until modern times, by which I mean the last few hundred years. For the sake of simplicity and consistency we can perhaps refer to this view as the 'Wrong View'.

Turning now to ethics – the science of morals – what does the Right View have to say? In this I am most familiar with the work of Immanuel Kant, whose beautifully lucid, profound and compelling arguments for the absolute, 'a priori' abstract and ideal nature of true morality makes his *Groundwork of the Metaphysic of Morals* essential reading. To quote from the introduction to H.J. Paton's excellent translation, this book's message "was never more needed than it is at present when a somewhat arid empiricism is the pervading fashion in philosophy. An exclusively empirical philosophy, as Kant himself argues, can have nothing to say about morality: it can only encourage us to be guided by our emotions, or at best, by an enlightened self love, at the very time when the abyss between unregulated impulse or undiluted self-interest, and moral principles has been so tragically displayed in practice".

Kant says basically that there are three kinds of 'good' – we use the word 'good' in three different ways and this distinction is central to my argument and so please excuse a short digression into moral philosophy. Firstly, we have good in a technical sense – a good pen, a good design, a good idea. These are good precisely in relation to the extent to which they accomplish practical goals or ends – we can say that this kind of good is 'ends oriented' or empirical, contingent upon results.

The second kind of good Kant called 'prudential good' and it relates to wishes or desires and emotional gratification, both for ourselves and others, in general as in 'a good time', or a good film, good conversation, or a good cause even.

Both of these kinds of good are relative to or contingent upon, worldly goals and the Wrong View of course holds that these are the only kinds of good possible. Whole philosophies of far-reaching impact have been generated by this view of the basis of morality – for example, Bentham's 'Utilitarianism' developed by J.S. Mill in the 19th century and currently in favour with, among others, the Conservative Party and its supporters – the greatest good for the greatest number with 'good' measured entirely in technical and prudential or pragmatic terms.

Kant's view of this kind of morality he makes clear. "Hence everything that is empirical", he says "is, as a contribution to the principle of morality not only wholly unsuitable for the purpose, but it is even highly injurious for the purity of morals; for in morals the proper worth of an absolutely good will, a worth elevated above all price, lies precisely in this – that the principle of action is free from all influence by contingent grounds (the only kind that experience can supply). Against the slack, or indeed ignoble, attitude which seeks for the moral principle among empirical motives and laws, we cannot give a warning too strongly or too often; for human reason in its weariness is fain to rest upon this pillow and in a dream of sweet illusions ... to foist into the place of morality some misbegotten mongrel patched up from limbs of very varied ancestry and looking like anything you please, only not like virtue, to him who has once beheld her in her true shape. To behold virtue in her proper shape is nothing other than to show morality stripped of all admixture with the sensuous and of all the spurious adornments of reward or self love. How much she then casts into the shade all else that appears attractive to the inclinations can be readily perceived by every man if he will exert his reason in the slightest – provided he has not entirely ruined it for all abstractions."

For Kant the moral law, the categorical imperative to act correctly in all matters is something necessarily true, just as 2 and 3 is necessarily 5 whether anyone thinks or believes so or not.

Now this Right View is not really provable in the sense of demonstrable or verifiable, and Kant acknowledges this. We are operating here at the extreme limits of human enquiry and our only tool is pure reason. "We can only defend" says Kant, that is we can only defend our rationality – ultimately explanations are impossible since explanations require reasons, reasons are causes, and eventually there are actions which are not themselves caused and so have no explanation.

These things – of which true goodness is one – do not exist in this world, they are timeless and abstract and as such are not susceptible to change, decay or corruption – 'goodness', which subsists in the 'four duties' – never to harm oneself or others and to help oneself and others whichever possible – is moral bedrock – the ethical gold standard.

The Wrong View rejects all of this. Morality is only contingent since nothing is abstract – morality is inevitably concerned with interest, interest in goals to be achieved, satisfaction to be met. Now I would say that this cutting loose from the 'gold standard' ethically speaking, has been the root cause of the major personal, social and philosophical problems of our time and this is the central theme, subject and key to this paper. So now, having identified and defined the nature of the problem, how does this relate to usury? Well, as I said before, usury must be seen not only as directly causing many of the social, political, economic and ecological difficulties and disasters of today – as we have seen and will see in the rest of today's seminar – but it must also be seen as a direct result of the abandonment of the traditional and time-honoured understanding of the fundamental realities of ethics and metaphysics.

We might even go further and suggest that the Right View was attacked and broken down deliberately and specifically to allow the introduction of usury on a large and 'legitimate' scale. This might sound like some alarmist conspiracy theory, but then again there were certainly enough people sounding a warning against usury and accurately predicting its consequences to suggest that those ultimately responsible for the new financial developments of the 17th and 18th centuries were not unaware of the implications of what they were doing and may even have welcomed them.

Again, if ethical principles are essentially abstract and imperishable, how can something immoral be re-negotiated by human beings? Can we decide that circles will henceforth be square, or that two plus two will equal five by the end of the financial year? But, of course, if good and bad, right and wrong, are only what thinking makes them, then to quote Nietzsche, "Nothing is true, everything is permitted", included all manner of injustices and selfish behaviour – as long as no-one complains too loudly, or as long as you can get away with it. A very convenient philosophy for usurers.

Although our main interest this seminar is usury, I think it is significant and worth mentioning that the change from Right to Wrong View has also resulted in problems in the psychological sphere. It has been argued that the modern individual has a different experience of himself from his ancestors, who knew that however uncertain and uncomfortable the vagaries of this world, the true world of eternity was a solid reality beyond appearances, a source of meaning and value in life.

Since men have made themselves the only measure of the universe people have experienced an increasing alienation and isolation from their world and from others in it. When individuals have to decide for themselves the parameters of their existence metaphysically and ethically, the ego finds itself thrust onto centre stage and suddenly strangely unsure of its lines. No wonder most people would prefer not to think about it; its not surprising that when it comes to education cuts the Philosophy Departments are the first to feel the bite of pragmatic government policy. Most of us just do not really want that kind of stress, and then we are all victims of the Hollywood Syndrome, we are all the stars of our own docu-drama, in my case it's 'The Life of Ibrahim', loosely based on the facts and also featuring in supporting walk-on parts and in descending order of importance, my family, my friends, my acquaintances, and only then everyone else in the world I'm not going to meet or ever be concerned with to any great extent, bit players on my stage.

When morality shrinks down to self interest – enlightened or otherwise – and psychology throws up increasingly alienated and confused mentalities, social disorders become inevitable, and America is probably the best example of the way things are going. Things are going west, and this is because we have for centuries been rejecting the Right View of reality and embracing the Wrong View at the behest of those who have most to gain.

And here I might just for a moment abandon the stance of resolute objectivity which I have been careful to maintain, and say that in my view, in the light of what I have mentioned of the failure of contingent morality to provide a workable basis for society, the Wrong View is certainly wrong; even though it is quite difficult at times to make moral judgements, traditionally men have turned to God for guidance, and Kant's controversial claim was that pure reason could confirm the ethical validity of God's decree in conceiving the categorical imperative, the moral law.

So to return to usury – my objection is not simply that usury is wrong because it doesn't work; because it results in practical difficulties, it needs to be controlled so it doesn't get out of hand and start producing all kinds of problems – which is the Catholic Church's current view of the matter, according to a recent Vatican publication on the problem of the Third World debt crisis.

No, it's simply the case that usury is objectively, absolutely and categorically immoral. Of course, unethical activities are the cause of undesirable effects, but this is not why they are unethical. When our society moved the goalposts, changed not only the rules but the whole basis of ethics by allowing usury in, then having accepted one form of immorality it was left with no solid defence against the breakdown of the whole moral order. We are reaping the results of this process today.

To finish I would like to give two examples of modern pragmatic thinking which I think show clearly that the answer to our initial question "What kind of society is it that not only permits but condones and actively encourages usury?", is that it is one that has somehow floated free from the moral 'gold standard', which has renounced Kant's categorical imperative, the pure impulse to do good for its own sake regardless of technical or prudential benefit and which is itself based on a knowledge and understanding of the necessary realities of the unseen, intelligible world and a reverence for its laws. A reverence which, Kant says, is the result of fear and inclination in equal proportion.

The first example is of one of the fundamental and inescapable problems for the pragmatist.

The other morning my children incurred my displeasure by pulling some large sprigs off a rosemary bush in a public planting outside a supermarket and attempting to sell them to passers-by at 10p a sprig. "But there's plenty of it", they objected when I remonstrated with them. "That's not the point", I said. "What if everyone pulled bits off the bushes, then they would be a terrible mess". "But they don't", was the inevitable reply, "and anyway if they did, it wouldn't make much difference if we did too, would it?"

This exemplifies in a nutshell what is known to logicians as the problem of collective action and to economists as the problem of public good. In the example you can see how the decision to pick the rosemary is rational, whether others do or not, and there would be little point in not doing so if other people were. If this is rational though – and it's held to be so – then everyone ought to do it if they wanted to although paradoxically no-one wants a ragged and vandalised public environment. The problem then is basically that rationally consistent self-serving behaviour is self-defeating, "the apparently rational course of action leaves people worse off than they need to be", to quote an article on the subject which appeared in the TIMES written by three Professors of Philosophy, Politics and Economics at UEA, which concluded that there was no rational solution to the problem even though it is frequently solved in everyday life. People do give to charity for example. In this case it would always be rational not to do so, since if other people are giving, your 50p isn't going to make much difference, and neither would it if no-one was giving. The paradoxical result of this reasoning is that there would be no charity at all if everyone took this position, although no-one would want that.

In brief, if other people are doing it, I may as well not, so then no-one does it which is a result no-one wants, we'd all prefer that everyone does their share. And, of course, no-one wants to do it by themselves.

This is the rationalism implicit in today's morality – it's empirical and pragmatic, collective action based on interest, rational, pragmatic self-interest.

The funny thing is that many people do want to take on public duties, even if the majority selfishly decline. Many people do refrain from picking the flowers or littering the streets – but why?

Plato's view, which he took from Socrates and which he held to throughout his life, was that injustice harms the wrongdoer, an immoral act has inevitably negative consequences for the person who commits it. All of us who recognise the truth of this in our deepest reflections, have accepted the Right View of idealistic realism as against pragmatic rationalism. This connects to our theme of usury as we have seen by virtue of the fact that usury sprouts in the fertile soil of pragmatism, that usury is now revealed as the fruit of the decay of idealism.

Usury is often defended by the claim that no-one would want or have any reason to lend money, which is a necessary part of social and business life, if there was no interest on the loan: that altruism and philanthropy – as moral qualities – are not sufficient motivation. I say this is a sceptical view of human nature – it certainly seems justified today, the dominant pragmatic rationalism as exemplified in the problem of collective action, cannot construe a functioning and complex economy without self-interest as a necessary condition, a 'sine qua non'.

This also means that the solution to the problem of usury is not and cannot be pragmatic, the solution lies in the recovery of morality. You see, the setting aside of usury would be a public good; unfortunately, left to himself, modern man cannot help but fall into the pragmatic trap.

The urgent question is then, why do and what can make people, co-operate collectively in the public good against their own self-interest? One solution has traditionally been a strong central authority controlling people's individual liberties to the necessary extent since many people are unable to freely restrain themselves – which is the only true and noble freedom – not anarchy or libertarianism, but the freedom to commit oneself to the conditions of being human.

Thomas Hobbes, an early English empirical philosopher, was stumped for an answer. "A power over us all" was needed he decided.

And with that intriguing thought I will go on to my last example, which I think shows how confused the present moral climate is.

It is taken from an article which appeared in The Guardian a short time ago under the title "A certain idea that the rest of the world may be wrong" – a confusing enough heading in itself, equating as it does the idea of certainty with that of the possibility implicit in the verb 'may' – we can be certain that others are wrong, or we can suspect that they may be – but surely we can't be certain that they may be!

Of course the heading is a typical Guardian play on words, so perhaps it is intended to echo the self-declared uncertainty of the rest of the piece.

Beginning with a reminder that the original zealots were the fundamentalist Jewish sectarians who killed themselves and their families rather than surrender to the Romans at Masada, the author, Geoffrey Taylor, goes on to ask "where does conviction end and zealotry begin?" On what basis do we decide the right and wrong of people's opinions and beliefs – when does passionate conviction in the rightness of our own views entitle us to oppose or suppress the wrong ones of other people? For this Taylor has no answer because, crucially, for him there can be no certainty in belief of any kind. He rejects indifferentism – which holds all value systems equally authentic, and nihilism, in which all are equally suspect, but can only suggest – in place of conviction – that we "distrust any assertion which expresses a certitude, and experiment for fruitfulness among those which do not" – practically a text book definition of pragmatism and typical I would say of contemporary ethics. And why is certainty to be mistrusted? Because "if certainty is unobtainable in science, which no-one now seriously doubts, why should we expect to find it in disciplines not open to measurement?"

My point is that ethics is beyond the reach of telescope or microscope, beyond any scope of measurement or calculation, beyond the grasp of logic or instrumental reason even – and it may be that we can be better guided by our hearts than our heads.

Certainly tradition has recognised the heart as the true seat of the intellect.

In conclusion perhaps I can restate my argument. The widespread practice of usury, defined as immoral economic transactions, is the result of the abandonment of idealism in favour of empirical, rational pragmatism. Certainly the development of the two has gone hand in hand.

There were three main causes and have since been three widespread effects of this shift from idealism to pragmatism; firstly, individualism and psychological alienation – the Hollywood Syndrome; secondly, socio-economic injustice, of which usury is the main symptom and political instrument; and thirdly, the loss of belief in intangible realities, the spiritual or 'unseen' world.

These three problems are part and parcel of a single issue. As regards usury then the remedy is not available to us unless we are prepared first to cure ourselves, we must not think that we can solve today's problems individually and out of context – at the heart of all the issues is the need for understanding, for good character and for correct ethical behaviour.

Well, thank you for your attention – I hope I haven't laboured too many a simple point or avoided too many problematical ones. My hope is that I have brought into some focus at least the ethical dimensions of the problems of usury and our society and hinted at the possible direction of a solution.

Ibrahim Lawson

Usury and Its Effect on the Environment: a Local View

AN ARTICLE in a recent issue of 'Natural World', the magazine of the Royal Society for Nature Conservation, begins in the following way:

> *"Let us get one thing straight from the beginning. The battle for the countryside has been lost. The struggle now taking place is a last despairing attempt to salvage something from the wreckage ...*
>
> *"Most of the old order – the great wetlands and woodlands, moors, heaths, hedgerows and flower meadows – have been swept away and replaced by new landscapes which are all too often dreary, disfigured and hostile to wildlife.*
>
> *"Endangered, damaged, lost, destroyed ... even in the dispassionate statistics of scientific record books the same bleak words ring out again and again. They are the sounds of nature being driven under; hammer blows for crumbling habitats and vanishing species...*
>
> *"Who could have foreseen 30 years ago that the countryside would be overturned not by urban sprawl but by the ponderous momentum of modern agriculture? But market forces, allied with new technology which can wring every last ounce from the land, have transformed the face of rural Britain. A triumph for farming, a catastrophe for wildlife ..."*
>
> *"The miracle is"*, the writer concludes, *"that anything has survived at all."*[1]

[1] See B. Jackinan and T. Paskell, "Nature in the Balance", in the Spring/Summer 1986 issue of "Natural World", RSNC, pp.13-14

The figures speak for themselves. Now in the 1980's in Britain, 40% of the natural woodlands have been lost, as have two-thirds of the natural coastline of England and Wales, 95% of the hay meadows, 80% of the chalk grassland, at least 30% of the upland grassland, heath and blanket bog, and over 50% of the marshes and wetlands, along with widespread pollution and canalisation of waterways.[2]

And this situation is reflected in every country in the world.

The above-mentioned writer puts the blame on the "ponderous momentum of modern agriculture", referring in particular to "market forces" and "new technology". Let us look a little closer at these so-called "market forces" as they apply to agriculture, and it will be apparent how usury, and this usurious economy that we have been talking about today, has its effect in ultimately destroying the environment.

I would like to take one example from Norfolk, the Broadland grazing marshes, which illustrates this process on a local level, and it is a process which is happening in greater or lesser degree all over the country, and for very much the same reasons. Small, locally-based farmers are being forced to give up traditional low input-output farming practices, which are conducive to a clean conservationally high-value environment, for intensive semi-industrial alternatives, which in their turn destroy the unique plant and animal systems which give the area its particular value and attraction. The reason behind them doing this is, quite simply, because the pressure is on for them to increase production so that everyone can get their money moving and pay off their loans, always with the extra pressure of

[2] See, for further detail, "Natural World", Winter 1985, RSNC, pp.24-33.

interest included, of course. The banks, as we have seen, have to get their money on the move in order for them to be able to make their own money and pay off their own debts. Governments have to do the same, for exactly the same reasons. Farmers, though, are not in a position to make money out of money. They have real wealth, i.e. land, which is finite and thus does not increase with regular increments of interest, and so for them to make money and meet their interest payments they have to increase production, whatever the cost to the environment.

The grazing marshes of the Norfolk Broads form an integral part of the Broadland ecosystem because they provide not only feeding areas for birds which nest around the waterway, such as herons and marsh harriers, but also because they provide the remaining large refuge, in their dykes, of the water-plant and animal communities now almost completely lost from the waterway itself. They now form the principal location for such nationally rare species as the Norfolk Aeshna dragonfly, which is confined to this part of England. There was also a Norfolk Damselfly, but that has already become extinct in England, having last been recorded from the Norfolk Broads in 1957. The area also harbours large numbers of winter bird visitors, such as Bewicks's swan and bean geese, sometimes in flocks of national importance, in addition to holding significant breeding populations of wildfowl, waders and other grassland nesting species such as yellow wagtail, for which the area is also of national importance.

These marshlands, after a long period of relative stability, are now threatened by further agricultural change. The traditional summer pasturing of stock has become uneconomic, owing to UK and EEC agricultural policies, and there is pressure on the farmers to increase productivity through deep-drainage and conversion of the land to high-yielding grass and arable crops. This means larger fields, reduced dyke lengths, and reduction of the dyke water levels. This inevitably reduces the area and viability of the present dyke aquatic-plant communities and their associated faunas.

The reasons why stock pasturing has become uneconomic lie in the political manipulation of agricultural policies, particularly those relating to subsidy and price-support, these manipulations all being, as we have seen, the result of, ultimately, the same economic pressures, only higher up the scale, as it were, as far as the Government is concerned. These policies have encouraged farmers in Broadland, and elsewhere, to take livestock off the marshes. Consequently cattle, the mainstay of the marshland landscape, are disappearing. At the same time, Common Market cereal producing policies are encouraging farmers to deep-drain and convert their grazing marsh to arable crops or high-yielding grass. The intervention prices of many arable crops, e.g. soft wheats, are now sufficiently high to give farmers a guaranteed return on the conversion investment, despite recognised over-production within the EEC.

In other words, despite the lack of need of the crop, farmers will grow it because it guarantees them a return, and they need that return to pay off their debts as soon as possible, especially since these debts are otherwise constantly increasing through the ever-increasing addition of interest.

Coupled with the operation of EEC agricultural policies are grants available through MAFF (the Ministry of Agriculture, Fisheries and Food) to help farmers improve field drainage. These grants range from 37.5% to 50% depending on the scheme chosen, and are awarded open-handedly without any formal cost-benefit analysis. If they show an increase over a notional period they are awarded. So, if the grant is of 37.5% there is another 62.5% which has to come from somewhere else, or, if it is 50%, there is another 50% which has to come from somewhere else, i.e. the banks, who will be more than willing to loan it since the crop is one which, with the present policies, will guarantee quick returns and allow them to reap their interest to pay off their own debts as soon as possible. And if anything should go wrong, they always have the land as collateral.

A further major reason for land drainage improvement is the obsolescence of many of the existing drainage pumps. Internal Drainage Boards have been unable to establish a capital fund for their replacement so that when a renewal becomes necessary they are obliged to seek MAFF grant aid, and, of course, to borrow the rest. These grants from MAFF, of 50%, are only available where a cost-benefit analysis shows improved agricultural production over a 25-year period. The remaining 50% must, as we have said, be borrowed, and the repayment and servicing of interest can only be met through an increase in the drainage rate. Thus Internal Drainage Boards, in order to attract grant aid, are encouraged to invest in efficient high-capacity pumps which allow for large-scale deep-draining, while the farmers, faced with a substantial increase in drainage rates and a poor return on stock, are obliged either to sell up if they are unable to adapt their enterprise to arable farming, or under-drain and convert.

What is important to note here is that whereas usury is clearly involved in the bank loans that the farmers, or the Drainage Boards, take out to make up the non-grant portion of the capital required in any of these cases, usury has almost certainly already been involved in the money which is being given as grant aid, since this latter is, of course, generally raised through interest-bearing bond issues on general funds raised at interest on the money-market by the government or authority concerned.

Thus both farmers and Internal Drainage Boards are seeking grants from the Government, whose money is already tainted with interest; both also need to borrow substantial sums from the banks to make up the difference. The Drainage Boards can only pay off their loans, with the extra pressure of interest always in the background, by increasing their rate of drainage, whilst the farmers, faced not only with this increased drainage rate but also the bank-instituted, national and international policies aimed at growing as much as possible of what will bring as quick a return as possible, are forced to continue to increase their production in order to pay off the debts they incurred in their conversion investment.

All this means that a combination of cash inducements, grants, and price-support, all of which lead to a further increase in the attendant bank-loans and subsequent burden of mounting interest, have led to a substantial increase of drainage and arable conversion on the grazing marshes. This in turn has led to a corresponding decline in the variety and ecological value of the land, along with the attendant problems of increased pollution. It has also led to a corresponding increase in the inducement of everyone concerned, whether farmer, Drainage Board, Government, or EEC, to become ever more deeply involved in the international banking system, which, ultimately, dictates the policies of them all.

A report prepared in 1982 by the Ecology Working Group of the Broads Authority, entitled "A Strategy and Management Plan for Broadland", commented on possible future changes in the following way:

"In considering ways forward it is important to note that farmers are as much the victims as the beneficiaries of present agricultural policies. Given declining profits, patterns of incentives and subsidies, and constant exhortations to improve production and efficiency, farmers are increasingly unable (and in some cases now perhaps unwilling) to manage their land to retain significant wildlife habitat and a varied landscape. They just cannot afford to. The imposition of planning controls on top of the present agricultural policies would only lead to further divisiveness within the community. What is called for is not swingeing controls at the farm level, but a radical rethink about agriculture and the role it should play in an environmentally sustainable rural land use strategy Without this we can really only tinker at the margins." [3]

Since 1985, the Government has agreed to offer compensation payments for farmers for them to retain the traditional stock farming on certain areas of the grazing marshes. This is being done under a three-year experimental scheme, the viability of which was considerably enhanced following designation of the Broads as a whole as an Environmentally Sensitive Area (ESA) in 1986. A large proportion of farmers in the eligible areas have in fact opted for this scheme, which guarantees them £50 per acre if they retain the traditional stock-grazing form of management. As a result, so-called drainage

[3] See "A Strategy and Management Plan for Broadland", Report of the Ecology Working Group of the Broads Authority, 1982, p.57; for further details of the above, see also pp.27-29 and 56-58.

"improvements" have temporarily ceased in all but a small fraction of those areas of grazing marsh which come under the scheme.[4]

However, if this seems to be a success on the part of the conservationists, one should remember that the basic agricultural policy of the Government has not changed, and, indeed, in the climate of the present usury-based economic system, with its intractable demands for ever-increasing growth and improved production, it cannot change. It just cannot afford to, as in the case of the farmers. What is happening in the case of the compensation payments is that a symptom of the disease is being covered up, while the main cause is being left untouched.

This, as we said, is a local example, but it is an example that is being repeated, in essence, all over England, indeed, for that matter, all over the world (the Brazilian rain-forests being an obvious example). The environment is being, or has been, changed for the worse, and in some instances destroyed, because someone somewhere wants a quick return, by interest, on money that he has lent, while someone else is forced to do something whose destructive impact he may well fully realise in order to get a quick enough return to pay back the first man what he owes him.

A Lakenheath farmer whom I met recently told me of a man he knew – another farmer – whose wife had come in one evening to find her husband in tears, with an empty whisky-bottle on the table beside him, – a situation in which she had never ever seen her husband before. When she asked him what the matter was, he said

---

[4] See, for more detail on the above, the Broads Authority's "Broads Plan" (1987), pp.40-58, especially pp.48-49.

"I had to mow that marsh", referring to a favourite piece of marsh that he had until then been able to retain in more or less its natural unspoilt form, but which he had now had to mow, and thus destroy, in order to convert it to arable. And this was solely because he was under pressure from the bankers to increase his productivity and thus his cash returns.

The point is that a whole environment makes for a whole man. Diversity in the environment makes for diversity in man. Diversity of species depends on there being pure air and pure water, and, ultimately, it is pure air and pure water – i.e. a pure environment – that are necessary for a pure human being, one who is pure both inwardly and outwardly.

The other essential requirement is pure thought and action, of which greed and the taking of interest are not a part.

Postscript

When the system of governmental price support began in 1947, farming was in a low gear; production was low compared with what it is now, and the costs were more or less in proportion. As years went by, successive Governments, under their own pressures of paying off money borrowed at interest on the world's money markets, called for higher levels of production, couched in the language of increased self-sufficiency.

In 1979 the "Food from Britain" campaign began, with maximum production now the target. But to get the highest output from the land, you must put in the highest and most costly inputs, and that means more money that has to be borrowed and more interest that has to be repaid, but if the increased output is there it seems to be worth it. The farmers went along with the idea of top-gear farming, but most of them did not have the surplus capital available. So they went to the banks, in their thousands, and borrowed millions of pounds more; their total indebtedness to the banks and other mortgagees went up to an estimated £6,000 million pounds where it had previously been less than £2,000 million pounds. Over-production did not matter. With the Common Agricultural Policy, farmers were guaranteed fixed prices as long as they grew the right thing.

The banks were happy. This agricultural policy suited them, since it guaranteed returns from the coffers of Europe. And in any case, they had people's land as collateral. In fact, the clearing banks and the larger merchant banks, which had been lending money to agriculture on an increasing scale, also spent large sums on advertising to the British public the advantages of the Common Market, especially the Common Agricultural Policy; and those who lent the most to the farmers were the ones who spent the most on advertising.

The banks were not the only ones who were happy. The agrochemical industry also knew that there was no money to be made out of low-geared farming, and that the more highly-geared farming became, the more the agrochemical industry could sell its wares. Its sales to farmers were but a few millions in 1946. In 1982, however, the value of such sales was no less than £1,350 million pounds. To buy such vast amounts of agrochemicals – as always, of course, with the aim of increasing production and thus immediate cash returns –

the farmers had to borrow even more, always of course at interest. ICI, one of the main companies providing agrochemicals, admits that this is its most profitable branch of activity and that it has become its largest. It has invested hundreds of millions of pounds of capital in developing its agricultural interest (to coin a term), and, like the banks, it too has spent large sums on promoting the present agricultural policy of ever-increasing growth and expanding production.

Thus Government grants and price-supports, which are themselves redirected money borrowed at interest, along with substantial pressure from banks and the large agrochemical companies like Shell and ICI, have combined to induce farmers to borrow ever-increasing sums to further increase their production. And so the spiral goes on.

Discussing the factors leading to a rise in costs affecting the bread prices in Canada, a leading Canadian economist, writing in 1975, points out another way in which usury enters the picture in its usual parasitic fashion. "Land costs", he says, "have already been discussed as a critical factor in the general cost-price squeeze on farmers … The main beneficiaries from land transfers are real estate brokers who on arranging a sale of a two-section farm on the Regina Plains could net $19,200 with a 5% commission. This cost must ultimately be added to the cost of food along with the payments of interest that follow the transaction.

"The cost of mortgage credit", he continues, "is the most inflationary of all farm costs. Based on index 100 in 1961, mortgage money was at 300 by 1975. The average farm debt payment was up to 400% in 1973 over 1961. These debt totals, reflecting the capital burden of land, machinery, and operating costs, represent a second level of production costs."

He then goes on to make an interesting observation, "Ironically", he says, "but not surprisingly, the level of debt burden is not reduced but increased during times of improved gross earnings. Farmers take on new commitments to expand at higher land prices and higher interest rates. Borrowing by farmers from other federally-funded Farm Credit Corporation increased by two-thirds in 1973 to a yearly total of $300 million, and short-term bank loans to farmers increased 21% in the first half of 1973 over 1972. This was during a year when gross farm income was up by 80% over the previous year!"

In this way the price of bread, indeed the price of wheat before it leaves the farm, carries, amongst other things, the added weight of parasitic real estate brokers, land speculators and mortgage companies, all of them basing their activities on usury.[5]

In this spiral of ever-expanding credit, production, and debt, it is the farmer who is under the most pressure, and when he is under pressure the land has to bear the brunt of it. It is the same everywhere. A report written in 1986 pointed out that United States agriculture was in the fourth year of a deep agricultural slump, with US farmers currently owing the banks a total sum of US $210,000 millions, which is more than the combined foreign debt of Brazil and Mexico. It was also estimated that a further 200,000 US farmers were facing bankruptcy in 1986.[6]

[5] See Don Mitchell, "The Politics of Food", James Lorimer & Company, Toronto, 1975, pp.63-64.
[6] See "Comment: The Common Agricultural Policy", Catholic Institute for

The operation of the EEC's Common Agricultural Policy has not prevented the emergence of a severe agricultural depression in Europe, either. In 1985, farming income fell by an average of 17.5% in the United Kingdom, and 5.7% in the EEC as a whole. Over the 1970's, with inflation and land values increasing, farmers borrowed heavily, as we have seen, to finance productivity-improving investments. Interest rates have been abnormally high since the turn of the decade (i.e. 1980), and land values are now falling. Lloyds Bank, which has loaned nearly 1,000 million pounds to the farming industry in the United Kingdom, estimates that 10% of indebted farmers will have difficulty in meeting loan repayments this year.[7]

So, far from improved production improving the farmer's lot, it is having the opposite effect. Such is the effect of usury.

Dr Yasin Dutton

International Relations, p.20.
[7] See op. cit., p.27.

The Oppression of Consumer Debt

DOMESTIC consumer debt in this country currently (1987) stands at about £34 billion pounds. That is, money owed by ordinary people who have bought things on credit but not yet paid for them. If private mortgages and bank loans are included as well, the figure is fantastic – £207 billion pounds. This does not include business loans or agricultural advances or government borrowing or any other kind of credit. Just outstanding private debts. This staggering sum is so big that it is extremely difficult for us to have any real idea of how much it is. To put it somewhat in perspective, it is about twice the amount owed by Brazil, one of the world's biggest debtors. But what on earth does this statistic mean? How does it actually affect us, the borrowers? What is its result in social terms? How has it come about?

Up to a few years ago, people did not get into debt unless it was absolutely unavoidable. The overwhelming majority of transactions were carried out on a cash basis. Credit transactions were basically limited to weekly or monthly accounts with local tradesmen which were certainly not interest-bearing. Loans could only be raised against tangible assets. The poor would take along grandfather's gold watch or great Aunt Mabel's gold brooch to the pawnbroker who would advance them £10 pounds against it. If they did not redeem it for £14 pounds after a month, they would lose their heirloom. The rich could borrow money from the bank against the security of the deeds to their property. The scale of debt was therefore very small. People would basically live within their means and only buy what they could actually pay for at the time. Then along came Isaac Singer.

Singer made sewing-machines. The trouble was that his cheapest machine cost $125 which at the time was a great deal more than most people could come up with at one go. He had a brainwave. Let people pay by instalments. He called this new buying method, 'hire purchase'. People paid $5 down and $5 a month. Within a year Singer's sales had tripled and within a short space of time he had cornered the market. The genie of domestic credit had been released.

It had now become increasingly possible to sell to ordinary people things which had previously been restricted to the wealthy and this is where the sinister side of credit creeps in. The more people who have something, the greater becomes the pressure on those who do not have it, to get it. It is a little like the example we had earlier of the enclosures. People had managed quite alright before, but the increased production brought about by enclosing meant that everyone had to get on the bandwagon or go down. The same thing started to happen with consumer goods. Fridges started off by being a luxury for the well-off and gradually became practically indispensable for everyone. The same thing happened with washing machines, three-piece suites, vacuum cleaners, televisions and videos. The pressure to have these things and others like them is overwhelming. Social pressure egged on by persistent and persuasive advertising virtually removes the element of choice altogether.

An extreme example of what can happen is illustrated by a conversation I had with a man in prison for theft. He said to me without a hint of guilt:

"Look, it's quite clear you have to live up to a certain standard. There are some things you've got to have to make life worth living. So I go out and take them from people who look like they've got enough." This attitude is quite typical of many of his fellow inmates. They feel they have a right to certain things and if the only way they can get them is by stealing, so be it. Two things we can learn from this are that advertising is effective and that crime does not always pay.

However, most people, thank goodness, are not so devastatingly straightforward. They do the next best thing and get these things on credit which, as you know, is all too easy. What credit really means of course is debt. Things have come a long way since Singer's time.

From the beginning there was interest written into the instalment plan so that by the time you had finished paying for whatever it was you paid considerably more than if you had paid cash. Even so the main idea was still to sell the goods and services involved. But gradually a shift occurred and manufacturers and retailers began to realise that they were making as much profit from the selling process as they were from the goods themselves. The nature of usury was making itself felt. Once the usurious process is set in motion, it is found that it is easier to make money from money, than from real production. Goods and services have now, in many instances, become a way of selling debt. The managing director of an Electrical Appliance chain put it bluntly: "In many cases there is more profit at the retail level in financing than in the sale of the goods themselves."

So you find it easier and easier to get credit. More and more credit cards become available. The impetus is not so much to sell the goods, but to use the goods to sell the credit. How successful the credit merchants have been in this country is reflected in the immense sum at present outstanding.

9% of most people's income is now spent servicing their personal consumer debt. That does not mean paying off your debt. The chances are that 80% or more of your income is spent paying debts. No, the 9% is just interest for which you get nothing at all in return. In other words, you spend over one month a year working purely for the usurers. In the case of many people it is considerably more than that and with some people interest payments account for 50% of their earnings.

In essence what people do when they buy on credit is mortgage their wages and salaries for an indefinite period. The implications of this are considerable, much more than most people realise, including for instance restriction of movement as well as the more obvious drawbacks but basically all is well as long as the money is coming in. When the money stops, as it increasingly frequently does, it is a different story. The obligation to make the payments does not.

In lower income families, 74% experience some kind of financial difficulty because of debt problems and 63% experience "real anxiety". Three hundred thousand mortgage holders are now three months or more behind. Last year 16,000 houses were repossessed by Building Societies and this year the figures are up considerably. This means that in the time we have been here today, fifty people in this country have become homeless through mortgage default. Seven hundred and fifty thousand credit accounts are seriously in arrears. Last year there were over two million county court debt plaints. These are just the figures. The real cost is in the stress and anxiety caused to people's lives and its accompanying toll of wife-beating, child abuse, mental breakdown, broken marriages, crime and increasingly, suicide.

So we can see that debt is not confined to the 'Third World'. It is much closer to home, probably – right inside of it. But the accompanying problems are exactly the same. The point is, it is not out there, it is right here. These things I have been talking about are the stark reality behind the glittering credit boom. These are the fruits of the usury which is both its cause and its only real beneficiary.

Abdalhaqq Bewley

Economic Imperialism

IMPERIALISM, or 'empire building', is about two things – money and power – and to all extents and purposes, these two are inextricably intermingled. Traditionally empires have been established by military force, military force which was used to expand and protect the economic interests of the emperor and his ruling elite. Later, as economics becomes more subtle and complex, the use of economic force begins to supplant military force which, however, remains in the background ready to intervene where sources of raw materials or markets for manufactured goods are threatened. This is the original IMF – the 'intervening military force', as well understood and employed by the infamous 'British Empire'. However, with the development of usurious economic transactions, specifically paper money and interest, the economic system becomes powerful enough in its own right to control whole peoples and nations. The raiding party, the punitive expedition, gunboat diplomacy, become things of the past. Incredibly, we are now witnessing a situation since 1982 where more money flows from third to first world in debt repayments, repayments of interest alone, than flows from the first to the third world in the form of aid and new loans. In 1985, according to Bob Geldof, Africa as a whole received $3 billion dollars in aid, and paid to western banks a total of $6 billion dollars. This bloodless imperialism would surely be the envy of all the great emperors of the past, and it is passively condoned by every one of us who refuses to recognise the fundamental immorality and criminality of usury, without which this bleeding dry of the third world could not happen.

The techniques of this new imperialism are really of secondary importance to us here today. From the Bretton Woods agreement to the unpegging of the dollar from the gold standard, from the influx of billions of dollars of Arab oil money into western banks to the lending of small fortunes to developing third world countries, from the failure of early expectations of economic development in the third world, the fall in the price of raw materials produced by those countries, the rise in interest rates, the manipulation of the currency market, tariff barriers to trade and first world farming subsidies. The result has been, as we all know, debt on a massively unprecedented scale. The IMF is now in the position of dictating policy to the governments of debtor nations and not just in the third world. This happened to Britain under Wilson's Labour government and the guiding principles are always the financial interests of the world banking institution.

Economic imperialism is a complex and multi-faceted phenomenon but it is all based on the twin pillars of fiat money and international credit with interest. In other words – on usury – and we cannot allow this to continue.

To finish this section I can do no better than to quote from an article from the Independent, 5th September 1987, under the heading "IMF visit sets hearts a-flutter" which gives a typical example of the nature of the activities of the International Monetary Fund.

"Last week, President Daniel arap Moi of Kenya expressed the hope that

the country's two state-owned banks would offer 30 per cent of their equity as shares to the public.

"The announcement quickened the hearts of members of the stagnating Nairobi Stock Exchange, and reminded everyone else that the International Monetary Fund, a champion of privatisation, had come to town.

"Its week-long mission here is the first of several to discuss what Third World governments call 'strategy' and what the Fund's detractors refer to as 'medicine'. Put simply, Kenya is running out of money again and is looking for cash.

"IMF calling-cards are common currency on finance ministry desks these days. Africa hasn't seen anything like it since the British moved into Egypt in the last century to oversee the Khedive's finances. And everyone knows what happened to Egypt's autonomy after that.

"It may be this historical precedent – colonisation following outside intervention in the economy – that African politicians had in mind when they labelled the IMF the policeman of the continent.

"Kiosk-owners, maize-farmers and street hawkers may not know what the IMF's initials stand for but they know it represents austerity.

"Zambia knows to what extent punitive reforms can erode national morale. President Kenneth Kaunda broke off negotiations on a revised loan agreement with the Fund on 1st May after rioting left 15 dead.

"Many multilateral agency officials privately sympathise with Mr. Kaunda, and agree that the Fund's demands for swingeing budget cuts, devaluation and a doubling of the price of maizemeal had brought Zambia to its knees.

"Africa's greatest economic worry is its haemorrhaging debt. At $200bn (£125bn pounds) it may not appear grave compared to Latin America's $400bn. But the burden for Africans has become intolerable.

"And, unlike Latin America's, the bulk of it is official, not commercial, *debt. In Kenya, for example, where annual debt repayments are 30 per cent of export earnings, servicing is considered 'manageable'. For Sudan, Somalia and Guinea-Bissau, where the debt obligation is more than the country earns in a year servicing is not manageable."*

Ibrahim Lawson

Summary

So, WE HAVE tried to give you a picture of usury. To define it in particular and in its broad effects. To show its historical development, and techniques, its philosophical background, how it determines the form of economic transactions and their consequent social effects.

We have given indications of what an economy might be without it and finally we have linked it with those urgent problems and issues that concern us today, to show its destructive effects in our global society.

We have shown that usury was never an acceptable part of human transactions. From the religious point of view it breaks the law, from another point of view it is unacceptable because of the imbalances that it creates.

In our own lives, daily involved in interest-bearing credit transactions – like mortgages, hire purchase agreements, credit terms in shops, deposit accounts in banks and all forms of paper money – it seems alright and everyone thinks it is alright. But it is not alright. It was previously abhorred. What was originally forbidden has finally ended up being a pillar of society, if not *the* pillar. Its effects were once seen and directly experienced. Its results are what we see of imbalance in the world today.

We hope we have given you food for thought. The preparation of this seminar was for us a journey in understanding. We would like with your help to take it on from here. We believe that there is in this a powerful, politically unifying critique that gives a common ground for all of us who are trying to address particular problems in our society.

Abdalhalim Orr

The Moral of the Story

THE ESSENCE of the usurious transaction is the endowment of money itself with worth. Once this happens, then, at first, a subtle pressure, later becoming a tangible force in every direction, pushes and pulls people to focus their energies on the acquisition of money. This *economic imperative* – the bottom line – does this get us more money quicker or does that? – becomes the fulcrum around which more and more major decisions are made within the usury-permitting society.

These decisions are not for everybody, however, because usury separates as nothing else can separate. It separates rich and poor, and teaches the poor that the way forward lies in becoming rich. Usury enshrines the notion that the purpose of life is to acquire money itself and at the same time it devalues the non-purchaseable qualities of character which usury-free societies used to value – especially because they can be the possession of anyone, i.e. honesty, integrity, courage, generosity, concern, humility, compassion, etc. and perhaps most importantly, contentment. And most important of all is the loss of the tranquillity that comes from an active, productive and non-frantic approach to seeking our means of livelihood. This has been supplanted by the acceptance and even laudability of a life-style of greed, selfishness and pride – an arrogant self-congratulatory praise of oneself as the ultimate cause of monetary success.

Usury is the transaction of guaranteed increase without risk. It is, after all, this pursuit of increase that is the essence of usury – a pursuit which never ends and that is directly opposed to the sincere expression of gratitude, gratitude based on contentment and giving the patience and reflection that allows concern to govern one's actions.

The possessor of money can acquire all that is desirable *that can be purchased* and because, of course, that is never enough then a lot of effort is spent to propagandise the illusion that what money purchases is all there is This propagandising is necessary to cover the hollowness of money-centred lives and to keep everyone looking in the same direction – towards the theatre of wealth possession and away from the wake of disaster and despair trailing behind the inevitable results of living exclusively for the purpose of gathering more money.

Remember the usurious society is a society with a lot of pressure on its members. Pressure to get more, to spend more, to want more. Pressure that leads to frustration that permeates every aspect of life. Pressure that doesn't leave time to consider any other purpose to life except to acquire, to have, to possess.

More and more people are tuning in to the theme of these seminar papers everyday. This is at once a heartening sign and also an indication that we had best be prepared for new and potentially sudden developments in the economic/money/currency sphere. The people who are profiting from the dominance of the usurious transaction are also aware that as the screws are tightened more and more people begin to question the validity of the present set of economic mores. Indications are that certain sweeping changes lie backstage ready to shift into position – one scenario might be the replacement of paper money and thereby the debunking of all anti-usury arguments which are based on currency/token exchange.

The ever-encroaching launch of EFTPOS (intertwined as it is with the 1992 European community changes) and its increasing scope is just such an indication. The Electronic-Fund-Transfer/Point-Of-Sale system completes the encirclement of the consumer and the removal of any necessity for him/her to actually physically possess their earned wealth at any time.

Direct electronic crediting/debiting of building society/savings/current/cheque accounts so anaesthetises the individual earner/spender that the intellectual investigation of the structural and ethical implications of this economic labyrinth within which they are caught would be even more difficult than it is at present.

The inspiration for the re-publication of these transcripts has been not only the very positive response and great number of requests received from people around the world but also our commitment to the belief that people want the best for themselves and their fellows. It is the shared belief that people want by their own intentions to live and transact in an atmosphere of good will and trust that directly opposes the climate of greed, mistrust and exploitation which so dominates the current global, local and personal transactions which we all are now engaged in.

Our central thesis is that there is another way to live within the world. Not at war with it, but at peace, and with a dynamic approach to our livelihoods that is also caring, empathetic and responsible to our fellow creatures and beholden to the generosity of our Creator.

The fact is that the people of good will must take action, and that their inaction is tantamount to surrendering to mistrust as the basic mode of behaviour for all mankind. Now that you are aware of our work and thereby we acknowledge your shared intention with us in this work, let me go one step further and call on you to actively enroll in the education of people to the importance of the abolition of usury: talk to people about these subjects, educate yourself and others about the corruption of currency, the control and infection of the profit-motive into every area of life, etc.

Mahmud Lund

POSTFACE 2009

Crisis! What Crisis?

THE CHURCH of England rolled out its big guns, in the form of the Archbishops of York and Canterbury, and trained both barrels on the perceived culprits behind the world financial crisis in a 'good cop-bad cop' duo where the 'bad' cop (Canterbury)[1] is so good that the 'good' cop (York)[2] is forced to be positively obsequious. Eloquent testimony to the mollifying powers of the English shires when even the plain speaking man from Uganda chose to address the gathered fraternity of international bankers in terms more suited to a Harrogate tea parlour than the fire and brimstone which their unbridled consumption of usury truly deserves. As he approaches the end of his speech one soon realises that the whole thing has been a genteel preamble to a request for a share in the proceeds of what his colleague (Canterbury) rightly describes in the Spectator as, "...that almost unimaginable wealth [which] has been generated by equally unimaginable levels of fiction, paper transactions with no concrete outcome beyond profit for traders." Our bad cop should perhaps take note that these transactions rarely involve anything quite so tangible as paper!

[1] The Archbishop of Canterbury, Rowan Williams. Face it: Marx was partly right about capitalism. The Spectator. Wednesday, 24th September 2008. http://www.spectator.co.uk/the-magazine/features/2172131/face-it-marx-was-partly-right-about-capitalism.thtml
[2] The Archbishop of York speaks to The Worshipful Company of International Bankers Dinner at Drapers' Hall London. Wednesday, 24th September 2008. http://www.archbishopofyork.org/1980

Enter now our 'rookie' cop, Norwich (Mosque rather than Cathedral). By limiting himself to citing the Jewish and Christian scriptures Canterbury is continuing to display the centuries old 'systemic denial', turning a deaf ear to the clearest and most fearless voice of all, that of the Muslims who constantly marvel at the refusal of their world-weary 'senior' colleagues to bring the accused seriously to book. However, as frustrating as this may be, the basic reason for it is very clear to us.

What else could we expect from an ecclesiastical organisation that rubber stamped the origins of modern finance at the very birth of the modern age and is thus complicit in its actions? What else could we expect when Christianity has abandoned the very concept that God might have anything to say about law, relegating that to the preserve of Judaism which it regards as an ancient 'law religion'?

As we have stood in prayer in the Norwich Mosque night after night throughout this recently ended month of Ramadan, listening to the entire Qur'an recited by heart by a young English Imam, we are reminded with a sense of infinite gratitude that we have immediate and constant access to something which our older colleagues do not and which they fail to recognise – the Qur'an. The Qur'an is the most recent in the series of monotheistic revelations, the last word in revealed guidance and warning against every form of idolatry; a later 'law religion' that was intended exclusively for this final phase in the story of mankind's struggle to conduct our life's affairs in the way that is best for us in this world and the next.

Therefore, returning to the case of the international bankers in particular and capitalism in general, it is well known in the Muslim world and increasingly so beyond it, that the Norwich 'rookies' have been shouting the charges from the rooftops for the past twenty years. We have pointed to the Emperor's obvious nakedness, we have described the ugly bits, taken his measurements and offered him a set of decent clothing. Until now he has preferred to listen to the flattery of his friends in Church and State but the chill on Wall Street is getting very uncomfortable. So now, putting all humour aside, we'll try again.

Our question to Archbishops Canterbury and York is: What happened to the religion of the man who threw the moneychangers out of the temple?[3] Or even more appositely, what happened to the monotheistic religion that said no to idolatry? How has it countenanced the open idolatry of money and greed that defines this age?

We conclude that Christianity's dilemma is its desire to do the right thing even though it is no longer sure what that is. But this lack of clarity has come about through its forsaking the revealed law, leaving to Caesar what is Caesar's, only for it to be inherited by the bankers who very clearly craft the law to their own ends by making use of whichever 'Caesar' happens to be ushered their way, be it Bush or Brown, Obama or McCain – or by simply taking care of things directly – after all, how often do the US Treasury's incumbents not come straight to it from the boards of investment banks? Christianity is left expostulating on the sidelines, as in the

---

[3] 'And Jesus went into the temple of God, and cast out all them that sold and bought in the temple, and overthrew the tables of the moneychangers, and the seats of them that sold doves, "And said unto them, It is written, My house shall be called the house of prayer; but ye have made it a den of thieves."' – Matthew 21:12-13.

case of our bad cop, or reduced to sycophancy as in the case of our good cop: "Let us help the moneychangers set out their stalls in the temple and perhaps they might be kind enough to give us a little for the temple's upkeep and for a few good works."

It is this impossible situation that necessitated the revelation of the Qur'an and the practice of the Prophet Muhammad, may Allah bless him and grant him peace, which alone among the revealed religions has an utterly clear articulation of what is not permitted in commercial practice, e.g. usury, hoarding and undercutting. Nowadays the Islamic prohibition of usury is known even to averagely educated non-Muslims. It also articulates a completely coherent set of profitable and permissible commercial practices, including modes of partnership, profit-sharing, crop-sharing etc., effective enough to sustain a vigorous global civilisation for more than a millennium until foolish greed and naivety made Muslims easy prey to the blandishments of duplicitous men with chequebooks and the offer of insane amounts of wealth such as can only be made when the means are no longer natural.

However, to the modern ear a word such as 'usury' rings uneasily. We think of Shylock and anti-Semitism, and if we go to the dictionary for guidance we only find it defined as 'exorbitant or excessive interest on a loan', that is unless we look it up in an etymological dictionary where we find that it is 'any interest on a loan'. The modern definition is of course, problematic, since what is exorbitant is very much a matter of fashion, it having been settled in Calvin's time as anything over 4% whereas today almost anything goes.

There is perhaps no better illustration of the authentic relationship of Islam to the religions that preceded it than this matter of commerce where it can clearly be seen that Islam is the confirmation of what was true in the previous revelations. The historically minded person, a dying breed, will discover that proscriptions identical to those of Islam against various business practices that have become common today were also to be found in Common Law, and have simply been expunged in the rise of the current commercial order:

ENGROSSING: buying up all of a commodity in order to control prices; monopoly. This is the very foundation of hypermarket and supermarket chains. The fact that a variety of organisations monopolise trade rather than a single body is no great solace for us who are squeezed by their depradations.

FORESTALLING: the act of going out to meet traders before they have brought their goods to the market. Another fundamental basis of supermarkets, who by the simple expedient of exclusive ownership of the market to which the traders are bringing their goods, no longer need to forestall the traders.

UNDERCUTTING: deliberately selling goods at cheaper prices than their competitors in order to take trade away from them and kill all competition. This is a form of barbarism which does not admit of a world in which everyone should be allowed to eat.

USURY: in Arabic *riba*, literally 'increase'; in general, any unjustified increase accruing to one party to a sale when stipulated as part of the deal, interest payments being one very obvious example.

This definition of usury has simply been left in the dust by the speed with which modern finance has devised means and ways of getting something out of nothing or getting more than it lent, for no effort, when the sum lent was merely digits entered in a computer terminal in the first place. They have gone to such extremes that the instruments of modern finance are simply not understandable even by advanced economists and bankers with long experience of their trade and are almost entirely in the hands of advanced computer programmers and mathematical theoreticians. This has resulted in the classic bubble phenomena and resultant collapses, recessions and depressions (not to mention the unavoidable inflation) that have dogged usury-capitalism since its birth, growing in exponential terms to such an extent that people are asking not whether there is going to be a recession but rather, whether it is going to be the final inevitable 'crash'?

Some of the fundamental axioms on which the pseudo-science of economics is raised include imposingly named concepts such as 'the law of supply of demand' which creates the impression that it is comparable to something like the law of gravity. This is one of their axiomatic (i.e. cast iron) truths that need no further proof. But the law of supply and demand is far from axiomatic, indeed many societies for great swathes of their history have not relied on it at all. Merchants, farmers, pastoralists and craftsmen knew the prices of raw materials, labour and any other costs and set their prices for finished goods or produce within well known limits whereby the usual level of sales would enable them to live reasonably well. The idea that you should charge a great deal for something because it is in demand leads to the logical conclusion that when there is famine you can charge a fortune for food, which is completely indecent.

The current situation represents the logical extremity of this indecency. People who have grown obscenely wealthy through derivatives trading and managing hedge funds, (which are themselves many multiples of the monetary value of the world's total GDP according to this new science-fiction view of economics) constantly seek out profitable uses to which they can put their intangible and illusory money, and so they buy, sell and speculate amongst themselves on commodities: gold, oil and now food, and thus we experience the rise in prices.

Supply and demand is not a 'law' but a strategic abuse of the market. Things have their values, and profits have their natural limits. This spurious 'law' is just one example of economics as a pseudo-science erected in order to justify theft. For middle class Westerners this is bad enough even if merely somewhat constricting, but for the impoverished wherever they are in the world, it is a matter of life or death.

It is clear from the above that the current crisis is simply the tip of an iceberg, whose causes are an enormous number of unacceptable inequitable theories and practices that are not only in themselves manifestations of an extreme greed that has burgeoned beyond all sane limits, but are arguably the very motor that is driving the destruction of the biosphere and is the machine behind the murder of upwards of a million Iraqis and tens of thousands of Afghanis in the ongoing fallaciously named 'war on terror', better described as a 'war of terror' which only the incorrigibly naïve believe to be waged for democratising the Middle East.

Now, our remaining options are few. We could 'tut-tut' on the sidelines like Canterbury and York knowing full well that we will be tolerated just as long as we do not seriously seek to impinge on the exercise of power in any substantial way. That would then be an endorsement of the entire enterprise, like the court jester who alone was permitted to mock the king as a way of disarming baronial ambitions. A safety valve.

We could campaign to bring this insanity to an end. However, this would be a duplication of effort, since, as we currently see, financiers and bankers are doing a very good job of bringing their own enterprises to an end, although they might bring down the last remnants of civilisation along with them. For the same reason, we see no particular virtue in taking up the armed struggle, they have already beaten everyone else to the option of violence. As for the ballot box, we need only look to the 'Caesars' we mentioned earlier to know what to expect from the vote. The very proposition that one is exercising a meaningful choice when presented with sets of candidates whose views of existence and whose actual policies are indistinguishable is laughable.

No, safety and security belongs to the people who embrace sanity, and that will comprise trading not with figments of the imagination but with real products and commodities and acceptable modes of transacting with them. But the madness that springs from assigning numbers to abstractions via shadowy mechanisms in the belief that this confers value must be seen for what it is.

Those who wish to embrace sanity will have to relearn what a just transaction is because it is no longer obvious – and they will have to make strenuous efforts to learn what an unjust one is, because as we have seen, opening the door to injustice, opens the door to greed, and opening the door to greed opens the door to idolatry and opening the door to idolatry opens the door to madness.

Many of the key elements that are sane and lead to sanity once formed a part of Europe's heritage, which she has by-and-large abandoned, but they are there in the last revelation from the Divine, the Qur'an and the concomitant practice of the Prophet Muhammad, peace be upon him, and the first generations of Islam, which endorses whatever was genuine in the previous revelations and whatever is wholesome in human affairs. These two aspects are coming together again in the large number of Westerners and Europeans who are embracing Islam earnestly looking for a way forward for humanity in a dark age.

However, when all is said and done, what remains abundantly clear is that neither church, nor synagogue nor state possess either the will, the method or the daring to face the consequences of embracing sanity because amongst other initially unpleasant things, that would mean embracing the fresh wisdom of the 'rookies' as well as acknowledging the source of that wisdom – the Qur'an and the Prophet Muhammad, peace be upon him.

Uthman Ibrahim-Morisson and Abdassamad Clarke

The Deconstruction of the World Financial Power System: an Analysis of a Different Kind[1] (2008)

To TRULY UNDERSTAND what is happening today in the so-called credit crisis, we first need to understand what happened back in 1910 when the Federal Reserve System was conceived and what the hidden agenda of the 'founding fathers' of the Fed were. Without an understanding of this historic background, we cannot possibly comprehend the deeper context of the ongoing crisis.

My analysis will focus on four aspects of the modern financial power system:

1. Fiat Money: how fiat money (or money made out of nothing) comes into existence.

2. Loss of Purchasing Power and Inflation: what effect the unlimited creation of fiat money has on the broader economy and ultimately on you and me.

3. Central Banks and the Fed: the hidden agenda and objectives of the banking cartels known as Central Banks and the Federal Reserve System.

4. Real Money and Shari'a Economics: the only viable alternative to the fiat economy.

[1] Delivered at the 11th International Fiqh Conference, Cape Town, South Africa, 18/10/2008

Please allow me some introductory remarks:

Even though, for reasons of simplicity, I will focus my discussion on the US Federal Reserve System, the same logic applies to all other Central Banks.

Although my explanations seem ridiculously simple, I can assure you that they are, technically speaking, 100% correct (I simply stripped out the bankers' language).

Try not to make sense out of all this because it does not make sense. Just think of it as your basic scam and you will be able to understand it pretty well, particularly in the light of the ongoing financial crisis which is beginning to take on historic proportions.

All of what I am going to talk about concerns you and me. It is our money and economic well-being that are at stake, it is our money and pension funds that are being used to bail out the banks. So listen carefully because the well-being of yourself and your family is at stake.

Many aspects of my analysis are based on ground-breaking work by other people. In this sense, they deserve the credit for the following analysis and not me.

1. How fiat Money comes into Existence

Fiat Money is money made out of nothing and comes into being through the creation of government, business and private debt. That is a very important fact to remember: fiat money is created from debt. We will later see why this is so important.

This becomes possible through a collusion of interest between governments and the privately owned banking cartels known as Central Banks and the Federal Reserve System. You might rightfully wonder how it is possible to create money out of nothing – the same money that all of us labour and sacrifice for our entire lives.

Let us use an example to best illustrate how fiat money is created:

It all starts with the government side of the equation. The government runs out of money and needs $10 billion USD to pay for its running expenses over the next few weeks. Congress thus goes to the Treasury and asks for the money. The Treasury official tells Congress that they must be kidding because all tax receipts have long been spent in January and February (most of it by the way on the Fed to service the government's debt). But don't worry, they say, and together they go down the road to the Fed. Now the Fed has been waiting for them since this is one of the reasons for which it has been created.

Once they arrive at the Fed, the Fed official takes out a big cheque book and writes a cheque for over $10 billion USD made out to the US government. At this point, we have to ask the legitimate question: where did this money come from? The astounding answer is that there is no money, technically speaking there is not even a chequing account, there is just a cheque book. This money came into being at the precise moment the Fed official signed the cheque.

It is therefore created out of nothing and is loaned to the government to be paid back with interest.

If you or I were to do that, we would go to jail. The Fed however can do it because Congress wants it to do it. We will later see why.

The Treasury official then deposits this new money in a government chequing account at the Federal Reserve System Bank (which is properly speaking not even a bank) and the government starts to write cheques to pay for its projects. Let us now follow a small part of this money to better understand what happens at the commercial banking side of things.

Once the money leaves the government side of the equation, it enters mainstream banking. Let us assume the postman next door receives a government-issued cheque for $100 USD and brings it to his commercial bank down the road. The bank official deposits the $100 USD and goes to the loan window to announce that $100 USD have just been deposited and the bank can now loan money. This makes everybody waiting outside the loan window joyous because this is one of the reasons people go the bank – to borrow money. Some people are however a little concerned because it is only $100 USD that was deposited. Do not worry, the bank official says, we can lend you up to $900 USD. How is this possible?

Let me explain: this becomes possible because the Fed has ruled that a minimum of 10% of all outstanding loans must be kept on deposit (this is called fractional reserve banking). Since 100% of 10% (in our case of $100 USD) is $1000 USD, the bank can thus lend up to $900 USD based on the $100 USD that was deposited earlier. At this point, we have to ask the same legitimate question – where did this new money come from? The amazing answer is the same – this money was created from nothing and comes into existence at the precise moment the loan is signed by you and me.

In summary, as a result of the government's need for $10 billion USD, a total of $100 billion USD have been created from nothing – all of it lent out and collecting interest for the banking side of the partnership. Interest on nothing!

There is however one important difference in the use of the money lent to the government and the money lent to us by the commercial banks. While the government uses this money to pay for its projects, the banks do not use it on their projects, but lend it to us for our projects to be repaid with interest and secured by our assets. While the larger part of our profits from this nothing-money thus goes back to the banks via interest payments, the banks will take all of our assets if we fail to pay interest on this nothing-money.

While the banking side collects perpetual interest on nothing, the fruit of our labour and sacrifice goes back to the banks in the form of interest. Whether in times of expansion or contraction, it does not matter: the banks always win – it was engineered that way. If we however fail to pay interest on this nothing-money, the banks take our cars, our houses, in fact all of our assets because we signed on the dotted line.

You might rightfully wonder how the banks which collect perpetual interest on nothing and have the right to our assets can possibly get into trouble as they do today. The answer lies in their excessive leverage (which is based on greed) where they lend out too much and keep too little in reserves. If only a few percent of the outstanding loans fail, the banks get into trouble because they cannot meet their reserve requirements – this is exactly what is happening today, which is falsely labelled a credit crisis. The current crisis was caused by an overextension of leverage while the tightening of credit is simply a side-effect of insufficient capital reserves resulting from this overextension.

For the above reason, the whole fiat system is a house of cards, and any major storm can bring it down. The higher the leverage, the higher the risk of failure. What we witness today in the so-called credit crisis is the result of an over-extension of leverage. This is the second important fact to remember; we will later see why.

2. Loss of Purchasing Power and Inflation

Let us now follow the diffusion of this newly created money through the economy. Since fiat money is made of nothing, every time new money is created and injected into the economy, the new money 'borrows' its value from the existing money and thus debases it. It is like pouring water into a pot of soup – it dilutes the soup. We experience this as a loss of purchasing power which is the phenomenon of inflation or, more properly speaking, the appearance of rising prices

I say 'appearance of rising prices' because in terms of REAL money (namely gold and silver), prices do not change over long periods of time. Rising prices (or inflation) are the result of 'making money out of nothing'. In ancient Rome, a one ounce gold coin (which is REAL money) bought you a fine toga, a handcrafted belt and a pair of sandals. Today, you can walk into any fine men's store and, with a one ounce gold coin, you can buy a fine suit, a handcrafted belt and a fine pair of shoes. In other words, the real price of these things has not changed in thousands of years. Real money therefore is the best protection of purchasing power, since it is not subject to manipulation (in other words, inflation) and thus ensures long-term price stability – something which our central banks proclaim as their core objective and which none of them have even remotely achieved. On the contrary, our central banks, by creating an unlimited amount of money from nothing, became the principal destroyers of purchasing power and enabled the concentration of wealth in the hands of a few exceedingly powerful institutions and individuals (through interest on nothing) while ensuring that everybody else gets poorer and poorer.

At this point, we have to ask another legitimate question: did anybody get our purchasing power which was lost as a result of inflation or did it just evaporate into thin air? The answer is: for every loser, there is a winner. Who got our lost purchasing power? The people who got the money first before it was injected into the wider economy. Who are these people? Obviously the government who got the first check for over $10 billion USD, the commercial banks which created new money based on the new money from the government and the people lining up at the loan window when the new money left the commercial banking side of things. These people got our lost purchasing power. By the time most of us receive this new money, it has already lost some of its value and is worth less and less. The losers are always us; the winners are the government and the banks.

Through the phenomenon of inflation or, more properly speaking, the loss of purchasing power, all fiat money is eventually destined for the 'graveyard of fiat currencies' (as proposed by James Turk, CEO of GoldMoney). On the other hand, real money (in other words, gold and silver) will always maintain its value and prevail in times of crises irrespective of governments, ideologies or moments in history. Why is this so? Because fiat money is subject to government and central bank manipulation whereas real money cannot be influenced by small interest groups and is only subject to supply and demand resulting from millions of people freely interacting with each other. This is why no interest group has ever been able to manipulate the value of real money and why government and central banks thought it necessary to move away from real money towards fiat money in order to manipulate the money supply. Why? Because they needed more money than they had access to. They thus debase the money's purchasing power through inflation and enable the exponential concentration of enormous wealth and power into the hands of a very few institutions and individuals.

No matter what anybody says, inflation is a hidden tax. Rather than increasing our direct taxes (which is not a popular thing to do and therefore not liked by politicians as the current administration in the US has demonstrated abundantly), governments prefer to take our money indirectly through inflation. This is why politicians love the creation of money from nothing and why they are in partnership with the banking cartel.

How can we as average citizens best measure inflation? Certainly not through the official government and central banks statements which put inflation consistently too low. While the US government and the Fed have pegged inflation at a few percent per year over the last six years, housing prices in the US have practically doubled between 2001 and 2005. As we have seen before, rising prices are a direct reflection of inflation or loss in purchasing power. In reality therefore, inflation in the US has been running at well above 10% per year as opposed to the official figures of a few percent per year we are made to believe.[1]

Another good measure of inflation is compound money growth (referred to as M1 to M3). While the European Central Bank still publishes reasonably accurate figures on compound money growth (above 10% per year), the Fed has stopped publishing such figures several years back – for good reasons – they would make even simple minds suspicious at the rate the US administration has been borrowing and creating money from nothing.

3. The Hidden Objectives of the Federal Reserve System

If we believe the official doctrine, the purpose of the Central Banks and the Fed is to stabilise our banking system and our economy. If these were indeed their true objectives, they do a very poor job at it and have consistently failed to meet their stated objectives.

These have, however, never been their true objectives. The true objectives of the Fed are fourfold (with the fourth objective underlying the first three) and are completely unrelated to their publicly proclaimed objectives. They are:

[1] The identical case can be made for the situation in the UK, and doubtless elsewhere.

1.   To consolidate and increase the power of the big banks on Wall Street (the exact opposite of what the Fed was supposed to achieve back in 1913).

2.   To reverse the trend towards private capital formation thus countering a trend in the early 1900's whereby corporations and individuals saved part of their earnings to invest in future projects.

3.   To arrange government bail-outs, at the expense of taxpayers, for those cartel members that get into trouble – a process that has got out of control in the ongoing credit crisis.

4.   To increase their power by buying influence through the river of unearned wealth generated by the first three objectives.

Now let us examine each of these hidden objectives in more detail.

1. The Money Trust

In the early 1900's, the American people and Congress were very concerned about the concentration of financial power in New York, which was commonly referred to as the 'money trust'. Congress set up a special committee chaired by Senator Nelson Aldrich to come up with new banking regulations to break the 'money trust' and disperse financial power away from New York.

In 1910, Senator Aldrich, together with six other highly influential bankers representing the financial empires of the Rockefellers, Morgans, Warburgs and Rothschilds, set out on a secret journey to Jekyll island and in nine days hammered out the fundamental principles of what would later become the Federal Reserve System. At that time, these seven individuals represented directly and indirectly 25% of the entire wealth of the planet. In 1913, the first Federal Reserve Bill, which was sponsored by Senator Aldrich (who later, by the way, became the grandfather of Nelson Rockefeller), was voted down in Congress because Senator Aldrich, who was the Republican Whip in the Senate, was known to represent the interest of big business.

This was however just a minor setback. They scrambled the paragraphs around a little bit and, on the insistence of Paul Warburg, added some excellent provisions to the revised bill that would seriously restrict the power of the Fed. When his colleagues asked him: "Paul, what are you doing? We do not want these provisions in our bill," his reply was classic: "Fellows," he said, "Our objective is to pass the bill, we can fix it up later." They then found two millionaire Democrats to sponsor the bill, spoke openly against the bill that they had themselves written, and got it passed two years later by a large majority except for some lone voices.

This became possible mainly because of these excellent provisions that were added on the insistence of Paul Warburg which finally won over the support of Brian Jennings (the head of the populist movement) who had previously resisted all efforts to establish a central banking mechanism.

And they did indeed fix it up later. Since its inception, the Federal

Reserve Bill has been amended over 100 times and all of these excellent provisions were long ago removed and many more were added that greatly expanded the power of the Federal Reserve. As we are witnessing today, the biggest increase in the power of the Fed is happening right now in the context of the so-called credit crisis.

Did they achieve objective 1? Yes, they did indeed. While there are big banks in the South and the West, these banks are nothing compared to the megabanks in New York. So they get an A on their scorecard.

I mentioned before that this meeting took place in total secrecy. When these seven men met for their journey to Jekyll Island at the Hudson railway station across from Manhattan (where senator Aldrich had sent his private railroad car for the journey), they were instructed to come alone, not to dine with each other on the night of their departure, not to greet each other should they meet accidentally and, once on the train, to use first names only (two of them actually used code names to increase the effect of camouflage). For many years after this meeting, all of these men denied that such a meeting had ever taken place. Only twenty years later, some of them wrote books and articles about what happened on Jekyll Island. Why was secrecy so important and what is wrong with some bankers going on a journey and discussing banking regulations? Ladies and gentlemen, these were the representatives of the 'Money Trust' writing the Federal Reserve Bill whose objective was to break the Money Trust! This is like inviting the fox to build the hen house and install the security system!

As one of them confessed many years later, should it have become known that these seven men were meeting to discuss banking regulations, it would have caused waves in Washington, on Wall Street and even in London. Secrecy, therefore, was absolutely essential, because otherwise their Bill would have had no chance whatsoever of being passed in Congress.

Before we proceed to discuss objective 2, let us now examine in more detail the composition of the group of people that created the Federal Reserve Bill. Around the table on Jekyll Island there were representatives of the Rockefellers, Morgans, Warburgs and Rothschilds. Is there something strange about the composition of this group? Ladies and gentlemen, they were competitors. Just a few years before, they had been beating their heads, blood all over the place, fighting for dominance in the financial markets of the world. Now these same people were sitting peacefully around a table and coming to an agreement of some kind. Does this arouse your curiosity? What was happening here?

To understand this better, we need to look at American history in the late 19th and early 20th century which is often referred to as the dawning of the cartels. US Corporations, which became big and powerful as a result of intense competition and, for this reason, were outdoing their European counterparts, started to form cartels to protect them from competition and loss of market share. It was William Rockefeller the 1st who said: Competition is a sin!

This brings us to the astounding realisation that the Fed is in reality a banking cartel. You will not find this interpretation in any text book. Contrary to the objectives of Congress who wanted to disperse and dilute financial power away from New York, the Fed has in reality greatly increased the power of its New York member banks. And to secure this increase in power, it has gone into partnership with the government – something cartels often do to protect their interests and secure their market share.

To camouflage the true intentions behind the Federal Reserve System, they then had to come up with an appropriate name for the sake of appearances. First they decided to call it Federal to create the impression it was a government operation (which decidedly it is not). Second, they added the word Reserve to make it appear as if there were reserves somewhere (there are no reserves anywhere) and finally they added the word System to create the impression that it was a system of twelve regional and equally important banks when in fact it was from the beginning dominated by the New York cartel.

From its beginning, the Federal Reserve System was based on secrecy, deception and misleading appearances. It is an appearance of the 4th kind: things which are not, yet appear to be.[2]

2. Private Capital Formation

In the late 19th century, corporations and individuals began to set aside part of their profits to invest in future research and development projects. This is called private capital formation. At that time, the

[2] It was Epictetus who said "Appearances are of four kinds: things either are as they appear to be; or they neither are nor appear to be; or they are but do not appear to be; or they are not and yet appear to be." (*The Creature from Jekyll Island* (lecture), Edward Griffin, http://www.scribd.com/doc/6479760/The-Creature-from-Jekyll-Island-by-Edward-Griffin)

banks were greatly concerned about this trend and tried to figure out ways to lure businesses and individuals back to the banks for the banks to lend them money.

They realised that the only way to do this was by lowering interest rates. You might say why didn't they just lower interest rates? From today's perspective, this is a perfectly legitimate question since the modern Fed has the power to move interest rates up or down, completely at their discretion. In those days however, money was still based on gold and silver and on that money there was no lever to influence interest rates. As we have seen previously, interest rates on real money (in other words gold and silver) were determined by supply and demand resulting from the interactions of millions of people. It was therefore impossible for any interest group to move interest rates up or down.

So they said that they needed a flexible currency to better serve the interest of businesses and individuals. What is a flexible currency? Ladies and gentlemen, a flexible currency is money made out of nothing. With this kind of money, it is completely in the power of Central Banks to move interest rates up or down.

This was the beginning of fractional banking. At first, they lowered the reserve requirements for gold and silver down by 30%, then by 60% and, under President Nixon in the early 1970, removed them altogether thereby finally creating a pure fiat currency.

By lowering interest rates, they were able to lure businesses and individuals back into the banks because everybody thought it crazy not to borrow money at these low rates. What people however tend to forget is that interest rates will also go up and economies not only expand but also contract. And when economies contract, interest rates tend to go up and people are pressed harder and harder to service their debt.

Did they achieve objective number 2? Yes, they did indeed. Today, most businesses and individuals are indebted to the hilt just barely hanging on by the skin of their teeth. Bankruptcies are at an all-time high, more money is spent on servicing corporate debt than is handed out to shareholders in dividends and the whole world is in a state of global recession.

Stock markets are collapsing across the world, individuals and public institutions, such as pension funds, see their wealth disappear faster than ever and governments incur debts at an alarming rate.

They clearly get an A on their report card for eliminating the trend towards private capital formation. As a matter of fact, as we can witness in the so-called credit crisis, our modern world is built on debt and the freezing-up of credit brings it to the point of collapse. While governments across the planet are busy bailing out banks, the next disaster is already looming on the horizon. As a secondary effect of the credit crisis, large corporations lose business deals because their customers cannot finance them, they find it increasingly difficult to meet payroll requirements and to service their debts to the banks. These secondary effects of corporate bankruptcies which are just around the corner will, in my opinion, be much more severe than what we are witnessing today in the banking sector. I am referring to the giants of the productive economy, companies such as GM, GE and Ford.

All of what is happening today came about because the Banking Cartel was so successful in reversing the trend towards private capital formation. They get an A on their report card for achieving objective 2.

3. The Game called Bail-Out

The third objective of the Federal Reserve System is called corporate bail-out. It works like this: if a bank or a large corporation is in trouble or a third world country which owes a lot of money to the Banking Cartel gets into trouble, the Fed goes to Congress and tells them that they have to bail out the bank or corporation because if they do not, thousands of Americans will lose their jobs and, who knows, the bank is so big that, if it fails, it might act like a domino and bring down all other banks with it. I am sure you can see the obvious parallels to what is happening today. Just switch on the TV or open the newspaper and you will be bombarded with the latest bail-out news from all over the world. Morgan Stanley, AIG, Freddie Mac, HBOS, and Bank of Scotland to name just a few.

Since Congress does not want to be responsible for all of these horrible things happening, they begin to use taxpayers' money to bail out the banks and corporations that are in trouble. The game called bail-out which started on a small scale in the early 1970s has since then taken on historic proportions and consumes funds which we cannot even begin to imagine – the zeros simply become too numerous to count.

As we have painfully learnt over the last few months, the European governments have just pledged $2.7 trillion USD of our money to support their ailing banking system while the US government has already spent some $300 billion USD on their crumbling financial companies and has pledged an additional 700 billions to be spent in the near future. Without even considering the commitments by the Russian and other governments, these figures are by any measure staggering, but will not be nearly enough to contain the current crisis (as the free-falling stock markets around the world clearly demonstrate). Once the full impact of the credit crisis hits the giants of the productive economy, such as GM or GE, corporate failures will grow exponentially and no government, irrespective of its fiscal policies and financial power, will be able to contain the mess and stop these companies from going under. At that point, the current credit crisis (which is still reasonably contained) will begin to mushroom into a global economic meltdown.

And the reason for all of this is the use of excessive leverage and the greed of the big banks. While governments bail out the culprits of this historic disaster without even punishing them, we are the ones footing the bill through massive inflation.

And nobody is on the barricades protesting – there is no revolution anywhere in sight. What is happening – are we all going to take it lying down or are we going to do something for our rights, our lives and the lives of our children? Ladies and gentlemen, it is time to wake up. If we wait much longer, there will be nothing left worth fighting for.

They indeed did a marvellous job of deceiving us and get an A on their scorecard for achieving objective 3.

4. Usury as the Key to Power – The Core of fiat Banking

Let us use a simple example to best illustrate usury and the effect it has on you and me and the world economy at large:

When analysing the construction of a house where $30k USD are used for the purchase of the land and architect fees and $70k USD go to the builder, we assume that the owner would then make a down payment of $20k USD and would borrow $80k USD on a 30 year mortgage at fixed interest of 10%. We calculate that the bank will thus earn $172k USD in interest payments on money made out of nothing (which represents 2.5 times what the builder gets for all the material and labour), and so we must conclude that this is clearly excessive and that any kind of interest on any loan of fiat money should therefore be forbidden.

You might argue that one should not forget the time value of money given the long period of 30 years during which the banks cannot use this money and the work and sacrifice that went into saving it. But not this money, ladies and gentlemen: nobody worked or sacrificed for this money – this money was created from nothing.

You now have to multiply this by every house, every factory, every office building, every personal, corporate and government loan, every warehouse, every piece of farm equipment, every ship, every airplane, every investment and you come up with a vast river of unearned wealth which is perpetually flowing into a gigantic lake of unimaginable wealth.

You might think these people get richer and richer and richer.

Not so. This is not the purpose of this money. This money is used to purchase influence and power. Once you have all the money you can possibly spend in a lifetime, what is left? Power! They do not buy the hardware, they buy influence. They use this money to buy the people and organisations that we depend on for advice and leadership. They buy governments, publishing houses, newspapers, movie industries, public interest groups, NGOs, political organisations, consumer groups, boy scouts, girl scouts – you name it. Any organisation that exercises any form of influence is a target for control. And the process has already progressed at an alarming rate.

In the so-called third world, this process has already been completed. These governments have already been bought outright and they could not possibly exist without this money. Ideologies are irrelevant – where is the money! The have used this money to turn inefficient dictatorship into efficient dictatorships, ineffective armies into effective instruments of control and repression. They don't care about the people whose standard of living has not changed one iota (if anything it went down); they only care about achieving control.

In that process, they not only pumped enormous sums into developing countries, they actually depleted the wealth of the developed countries which is also part of the plan. In many ways they simply waste money to artificially lower our living standards. A strong country will resist control. A weak country however, where people are hungry and have no shelter, will be much easier to control.

Now we have to ask another legitimate question: what, if anything, can we still do?

4. Shari'a[3] Economics and Real Money

First, we obviously have to move away from fiat money (money made out of nothing) towards real money (money with intrinsic value). Why is this so important? Because the core function of money is that of a temporary store of value to preserve purchasing power over long periods of time, and fiat money is simply a terrible store of value as recent history has shown us again and again. Just think of what happened to the Reichsmark after World War II – it devalued to nothing in a matter of months.

Real money: today, the increasing influence of speculative investors in the bullion market projects a distorted picture of wild swings in the 'price' of bullion (as measured in paper currencies). In the past, when gold and silver were currencies, their inflation-adjusted price in terms of today's dollars did not change over long periods of time. The only changes in the 'price' of bullion resulted from changes in supply and demand patterns. This happened for example when Christopher Columbus discovered the Americas, thereby enabling the massive 'repatriation' of gold and silver to Europe and thus increasing the supply side within a stable demand environment. The obvious result was a slow and gradual decline in the inflation-adjusted paper value of bullion over several hundred years.

---

[3] *Shari'a* – 'Islamic law' – derives from a word meaning a 'road' particularly one in the desert leading to water.

Only when true fiat currencies came into being in the 20 century (before that, all fiat currencies were at least fractionally backed by gold and silver), did the price of bullion become exposed to rapid fluctuations. These fluctuations in the paper-value of bullion are the direct result of the diminishing role of gold and silver as currency:

In 1477 (before the discovery of the Americas), bullion prices were at their highest: an ounce of silver stood, inflation-adjusted, at $806 USD and an ounce of gold at $12,000 USD (historically, the gold/silver ratio varied narrowly between ¹⁄₁₅ and ¹⁄₁₆)

In 1992, an ounce of silver stood at $4.7 USD, an ounce of gold at $270 USD and the gold/silver ratio was ¹⁄₅₇.

I am often asked how gold and silver can be used as investment instruments. This question reveals a basic misconception of the role of bullion and stems from our focus on interest-based and speculative profits where money is used to make money. Gold and silver are stores of value and not investment instruments. It is thus not possible to earn a 'return' on gold and silver[4]. It is however possible to protect one's wealth over extended periods of time without fear of loss of purchasing power.

What does this mean for *halal*[5] investment practices?

First, it implies the use of REAL rather than fiat money. In the

[4] Except in trade through profit-and-loss sharing investments, which are active means of putting gold and silver to work rather the passive expectation of a return on money that modern people expect and to which the author refers. Ed.
[5] *Halal* is 'permissible', and is often coupled with 'wholesome'.

Qur'anic perspective, all fiat money is *haram*[6] — only money with intrinsic value is *halal* and it must be based on gold and silver.

Secondly, we have to move away from commercial banking practices to *Shari'a*-compliant investments. Why? Because first and foremost, *Shari'a* economics forbids the use of money to make money! What does this imply?

It means for example that more than $600 trillion USD worth of derivatives, which represent almost 20 times the monetary value of annual global economic output, should be redirected to the productive economy because today these instruments are exclusively used to make money with money (which is *haram* and forbidden).

Just imagine for a moment what would happen if only a small part of this money were invested in production and trade (at present, only a few trillion USD out of the global money supply of more than $600 trillion USD flow into the productive economy). This would mean that ordinary people would finally reap the benefits of their labour and risk-taking and that the flow of global capital would reverse and come out of the hands of a very few into the hands of the many.

Today, production has been largely outsourced to developing countries to take advantage of cheap labour costs and is widely considered 'dirty' and inessential for developed economies. Free trade (whatever little of it is left in the face of the globally monopolised and cartelised flow of goods) has been relegated to a form of tourist attraction for developing and third-world economies.

---

[6] *Haram* is impermissible.

In our modern economies, the vast majority of all profit is made either by using money to make money (i.e. through bets in the form of derivatives where one can even bet on the weather or how soon Barack Obama is going to be killed once president – apart from being sickening, this is worse than Roulette) or by collecting interest on 'nothing-money' loaned to governments, businesses and individuals. It is a total reversal of the historic role of money diverting it away from the productive economy to a purely financial economy. The economy of modern power centres such as London or New York is mostly reduced to money making money. In these modern power centres, one looks in vain for industrial production or free trade – attributes which used to be the hallmark of power centres of the past.

We therefore need to turn away from the financial to the productive economy and must reverse the harmful trend of using money to make money.

Second, *Shari'a* economics forbids interest-based loans, all of which are considered usurious, no matter what the level of interest. Let me explain this in more detail since I get a lot of questions on this point. In an interest-based loan, the lender gets an undue advantage (or increase) because of the interest paid by the borrower. There is undue increase with one side of the equation getting the short end of the stick. This is why such loans are *haram*.

This implies that the core business of modern banking (both commercial and Islamic banking), namely the risk-free loaning of 'nothing money' in return for repayment plus interest or guaranteed profit, is *haram*: first because the banks use money created from nothing to generate a massive and risk-free inflow of unearned wealth, and second, because any risk-free profits have been forbidden since Biblical times and the Qur'anic revelation (please note that most so-called Islamic instruments are as risk-averse as their commercial counterparts).

What then are Shari'a-compliant investments?

As we have seen before, Shari'a-compliant investments must be based on REAL rather than fiat money. Some people argue that any commodity with intrinsic value can serve as real money. Although this is correct from an academic point of view, most commodities, with the exception of bullion and oil, do not own one essential attribute of real money: they are not universal. Since oil is rather difficult to store for an average person and the only precious metals available in sufficient quantities to serve as money are gold and silver, the choice is self-evident.

Secondly, it implies that all forms of financing must be based on shared profit/risk schemes where the investor participates in the gain or loss of a project together with the 'borrower' and where the 'borrower's' seed assets are protected against expropriation. All types of modern loans therefore do not qualify. In interest-based banking, all collateralised assets go to the lender once interest payments on a loan cannot be maintained (as we all know very well and might have experienced ourselves), and the borrower loses his or her assets. In Shari'a-compliant investments, this could never happen.

Shari'a-compliant investments therefore must always be based on shared profit and risk and must extend into the productive rather than the financial economy. This is the core attribute of Shari'a-compliant investments, and on that attribute, we need to reconstruct a new understanding of what correct financial investments really mean.

To close our discussion, we need to consider what we as average citizens can do about all this. In a very direct way, all of us can combat the usurers by not borrowing money from them and by putting pressure on our respective governments to increase their fiscal responsibility and reign in their long-term obligations to the banking cartel (because they incur debts on our backs). This is how all of us can together begin to erode their power-base and eventually bring them to their knees. Why? Because the creation of all fiat money starts with debt – in the absence of debt, fiat money cannot be created. Remember that in the very beginning of my talk I pointed out that fiat money comes into existence through the creation of debt.

Ladies and gentlemen, we still have time to do something. Even though time is quickly running out, we can still meet as we do; we are still free to discuss the deconstruction of the world financial system and the abolition of central banking. But time is quickly running out. If we continue to wait on the sidelines, we play into their hands. Ladies and gentlemen, it is an all-out war without mercy or consideration for the enemy. If we don't do something, we will most certainly become the victims. As one of the founding fathers of the US constitution is on record as saying: why stand we here idle when our brethren are already in the field?

Dr. Zeno Dahinden

Open Trade – A Call to Action

AFTER the seminar *Usury: the Root Cause of the Injustices of our Time* in 1987, the first impulse was to move to action. The result was the foundation of the organisation PAID: People Against Interest Debt, which aimed at both raising consciousness of the pivotal part that usury has played in history (and which it continues to play in the world today) as well as campaigning against it.

The bold call of PAID for mediums of exchange with real intrinsic value and a non-usurious economy saw fruition with the pioneering work of Umar Vadillo as the first steps were taken towards the minting of gold and silver currency and the demonstration of their use at unique open markets organised for the purpose.

This is precisely what took place in Birmingham UK at the Fair Trade Fair of October 1992 at which gold and silver coins, specially minted for the occasion, were introduced to a fascinated public by Abdalfarid Bermejo, the leader of the Spanish Muslims. Umar Vadillo arrived with a group of Spanish traders bearing trading goods from Spain and N. Africa under profit-and-loss sharing contracts, while a group came likewise from London with a parallel set of newly minted silver coins.

Since that pivotal event, open markets have been organised biennially in Mertola (Portugal), annually in Monastir (Spain) and Norwich (UK), four times a year in Potsdam (Germany), and Köln (Germany), Granada (Spain) and further afield.

Apart from Spain and the UK, coins have since then been minted in Dubai, Malaysia (by the Royal Malaysian Mint during the premiership of Dr Mahathir bin Mohamad and subsequently) and in Indonesia.

In both these latter countries there has been a great deal of inspirational work in the establishment of the usage of the gold dinar and silver dirham, particularly in Indonesia with their *wakala* institutions[1] for the exchange of the coins and open market/trading initiatives. They have also founded JAWARA[2] (Gold Dinar and Silver Dirham Users' Network of Nusantara) which is a network of both individuals and institutions accepting the bi-metallic coins as a medium of exchange in everyday transactions.

In Malaysia, Umar Vadillo, as of this writing (spring 2009), is actively promoting the full implementation of a non-usurious economy employing gold and silver coins with the full support of the state of Kelantan, with other states in Indonesia ready and waiting to do the same.

Trading is a vital part of any and every culture, and is intrinsic to the health of those cultures and their relations with each other. It is arguably the oldest human activity, predating law and governance. It is carried on between nations both in times of war and in peace, and is the basic means by which any society ensures the acquisition, exchange and distribution of goods, services and resources.

We have coined the term 'open trade' to denote healthy and

---

[1] http://wakalanusantara.com/
[2] http://www.jawaradinar.com

transparent commercial practices free of systemic usury or other inequities, concealed or otherwise. There is a fundamental difference in intention between modern capitalism and open trade; capitalism is predicated on the assumption that if government provides opportunity for capital, the market in turn will provide for everyone else, which is called the 'trickle-down' effect. However, this is demonstrably not working.

The first duty of government is to ensure that there is a just environment within which people may be free to pursue their livelihoods in a manner that benefits them. The objective cannot be for the state to feed, clothe and house its people; that would always have disastrous implications for taxation and result in an over-bloated state permanently hungry for resources. Government must provide an open economic environment within which people are free to pursue trade and other forms of business. It must ensure the maintenance of the justice necessary to protect the weak from the excesses of the rich and powerful and to ensure that short-term political expediency does not result in long term corruption and oppression.

The following outline of open trade is derived from societies founded on the establishment of just trading environments, and embodies principles that recognise and encourage people's natural motivation to acquire wealth and resources in the world, contrary to the modern business environment that places sometimes impassable obstacles of capital requirements in front of the aspiring entrepreneur, requirements that force the businessman into the trap of the banks from the very first day.

Open trade is a term intended to cover a variety of forms of trade and business practice that are in themselves just, intrinsically healthy and life-affirming. They are not just solutions to problems, not even to the problem of usury, but are the opposite of the injurious, unjust and malignant practices that characterise the capitalism of our time.

1. Open Currencies – gold and silver coins

The first and most important element of open trade is to restore real currencies, which can include any commodity of genuine value that people agree on using, whether on a local scale, over a wider area or even globally. Nevertheless, there is no doubt that wherever people have had the freedom to make this choice, they have most often chosen gold and silver, and so the importance of gold and silver coinage for open trade is considerable. There are many historical examples that show that gold has suffered no inflation at all in two millennia, as we saw in the essay by Dr Dahinden. This will prove very significant for people tired of seeing their wealth silently eaten away by the deteriorating effects of inflation. This will prove doubly significant for people who simply cannot understand how billions and trillions can be wiped off the stock market overnight and vanish.

2. Open Markets

The second key element of open trade is the establishment of free and open markets in which any enterprising person may trade, so long as they observe simple laws preventing the incursion of exploitative modalities. Therefore, no shop may be erected in these markets (although shops are permitted outside of its precincts under certain conditions), and no rent may be charged from traders nor levies taken from their trade. This does not preclude traders from contributing to the ordinary running costs of the market. Such markets are 'endowments' and, once established, may not be impinged upon in any way that detracts from or alters their fundamental purpose.

After a sound currency, there is probably no initiative that would have a more profound effect on the everyday life of millions of people than the institution of such markets because of the extraordinarily liberating opportunity they provide for ordinary people to go out in the morning and sell their wares at no additional cost to themselves. Modern man is oppressed by the artificially imposed necessity to lease commercial properties and pay local government rates to such an extent that this damages trade itself, damages the ability of ordinary people to engage in gainful activity, ironically rendering millions of people a burden on the welfare state due to 'unemployment'.

Open markets while potentially depriving the state of revenue would also remove from the shoulders of an ever-decreasing pool of taxpayers the intolerable burden of a passive workforce waiting for handouts or needing coercion of various sorts into productive economic activity.[3]

[3] It is also vital to remember invisible, non-economic, social and community-building aspects of the market. *See* "Markets as social spaces", Sophie Watson and David Studdert, http://www.jrf.org.uk/publications/markets-social-spaces, a study of the Open University, published by the Joseph Rowntree Foundation.

3. Contracts

The third important element is the revival of contracts such as profit-and-loss sharing, trade investment contracts, and partnership manufacturing contracts. This must be preceded by the identification of the wrong and unjust modes of contracting in order to avoid them, e.g. undercutting, regrating, engrossing, forestalling[4] and usury. We have seen in Aisha Bewley's magisterial essay that Venice in its heyday and Ottoman society were two examples of societies that were funded by profit-and-loss sharing investment in trade contracts. Thus, these contracts as proposed here are not experimental innovations thought up by idealistic dreamers – we cannot afford the endless cycle of idealism followed by disillusionment – but taken direct from civilisations known to have thrived for centuries on the practice of non-usurious trading modalities.

4. Open Production

The fourth element is the revival of open production in a social rather than competitive and individualistic way. Along with creating bodies that maintain high quality standards, care for members' welfare needs and a whole raft of other aspects of social welfare, we need them to engage in the education of the young in useful skills on-the-job rather than in institutions of learning, however necessary the latter are. Examples of such bodies have been the various guild institutions, in both East and West, before they went into decadence and decline.

---

[4] http://en.wikipedia.org/wiki/Regrating

Among their pivotal activities were helping manufacturers in their needs to raise capital, for example, to update equipment or increase stock. Because of this the guilds were seen as competitors by the emerging banks and the new fiscal state, and therefore they had to be absorbed or done away with altogether. Subsequently, their history has been rewritten in a fashion that precludes modern man rediscovering this dynamic social institution. However, as long as we remain unaware, we are doomed to be passive employees of the increasingly monopolistic corporate world and passive citizens of an increasingly intrusive state. But as we have seen, corporate gigantism is ultimately untenable. So the human scale and social responsibility of the guild will return to centre stage as matrix for manufacture in the future just as it has been for a major part of history.[5]

5. Open Distribution

The fifth element is the establishment of open distribution rather than the closed and monopolistic distribution networks of today. Open distribution will occur via groups of manufacturers, producers and traders or their agents transporting their goods and products to open markets further afield, as opposed to being part of the monopolistic distribution channels which are very largely controlled by supermarkets and other brand-name chain-stores, or by privately owned networks of warehouses, wholesalers and hauliers.

The corporate world with its ownership of the modern retail market space, allows itself the privilege of moving products between

[5] Vadillo, Umar; *The Return of the Guilds*, http://www.bogvaerker.dk/guilds.html

its various outlets just as its buyers dictate the terms on which it acquires the commodities that go into its goods and shifts its manufacturing to the most cost-beneficial 'labour markets' around the world. Open distribution and open markets form the real outlet for the natural partnerships and transactions between producers, investors and entrepreneurial traders that are the engine behind the movement of merchandise. The trader will find his natural partner in the investor who will lend him, on a profit-and-loss sharing basis, the funds to buy and move goods between markets.

6. Endowments

The sixth element is the endowments which, although not aspects of trade in themselves, determine so much of the society in which trade happens. The endowments are inalienable properties which are dedicated, either in their use or the income derived from them, to charitable and educational purposes. In most traditional societies before the rise of the modern welfare state, welfare and social needs were catered for by these means.

The welfare state is based on loans from banks, the servicing of which ultimately make its purposes unachievable, as we see today with the progressive dismantling of hard-won free medical and educational services, the disappearance of pension funds and the clear admission that there is no solution to the problem of the ageing population.

The endowments are based on the reliable productivity of land, so that in some historical contexts, such as nineteenth century

Ottoman society, almost two-thirds of real estate was held in the form of private endowments devoted to such charitable purposes as hospitals, soup-kitchens, educational establishments for every section of society and endowments to take care of the natural environment in various ways that are hard for modern man to conceive of, so radical are they. For example, one such charity was dedicated to taking care of migratory storks, which through exhaustion had to interrupt their migrations. Another was dedicated to looking after and feeding hungry wolves in the hills of Anatolia.[6]

Such endowments meant that society as a whole was not engaged in a Darwinian struggle for survival but rather was able to give the fullest expression to its most creative and altruistic instincts since basic needs were taken care of. Naturally such a view of existence does not suit banks and the modern state which saw to the demise of endowments by the simple expedient of seizing them. This was then followed up with a series of studies purporting to show them as weakening and pacifying the population, contrary to the dynamic activity created by banking. However, a cynical view might suggest that this apparent dynamism consists of modern men and women running furiously to service their debts, just to stay in the same place.

This list is not exhaustive but covers some of the indispensable aspects of genuine open and fair trade. Although we have referred to past practice and history, there is no sense in which these elements are recovered by 'going back in time' or 'turning the clock back'.

[6] For a more detailed picture of the actual institution in Ottoman society of endowments see the chapter "Waqf", by Prof. Mehmet Maksudoglu, in *Sultaniyya*, Shaykh Abdalqadir as-Sufi, Madinah Press 2002, Madinah Press, ISBN: 0-620-29054-5.

The fact of their practicability in actual historical societies means that we are not yet again positing 'ideas' and 'ideals' since this has been the bane of the modern world as we discover, often traumatically, the defects of our ideas. Rather, as the inevitable contradictions of a usurious economy break down society, we will discover that these elements were indeed formed to stand the test of time, and indeed, we are well advised to be active in their recovery now.

Abdassamad Clarke

Bibliography

Modem Works

The Creature from Jekyll Island: A Second Look at the Federal Reserve, G. Edward Griffin, Amer Media; 4th edition, June 2002.

The Debt Threat, Tim Congdon, Blackwell. 1989.

Aid as Imperialism, Teressa Hayten, Catherine Watson. Pluto Press. 1989.

Blood in the Streets: Investment Profits in a World Gone Mad, James Dale Davidson, Sir William Rees-Mogg. Sidgwick Softbooks. 1989.

For the Coming Man, Shaykh Abdalqadir al-Murabit, Murabitun Press. Norwich UK. 1988.

Interest and Inflation-free Money, Margrit Kennedy, Permaculture Institute Publications. Steyerberg, W. Germany. 1988.

New Internationalist Magazine, No.168 Feb. 1987, Money makes the World Go Round, also No.171 May 1978, Grow Your own Dollars.

The Sane Society, Erich Fromm, Routledge & Kegan Paul 1956, Chapter on 'Man in Capitalistic Society'.

Debt Shock, Darrell Delamide, Weidenfeld & Nicolson 1984.

The Man Who Stole Portugal, by Bloom.

The Moneylenders, Anthony Sampson, Hodder and Stoughton, London 1981.

Buy Now, Pay Later, Hillel Black, Morrow & Co., New York 1961.

End of Economics: Islamic Critique of Economics, Umar Vadillo, Madinah Press, 1991.

Return of the Gold Dinar, Umar Vadillo, Bookwork, Norwich, UK, 1996.
Fatwa on Banking, Umar Vadillo, http://www.scribd.com/doc/6418291/Fatwa-on-Banking

Historical Perspectives

17th Century Economic Documents, Eds. Thirsk and Cooper, Oxford University Press 1972.
A Discourse upon Usury, by T. Wilson. Introduction, R.H. Tawney, Kelley, New York 1963.
Tudor Economic Documents, Eds. Tawney and Power, Longmans Green 1924, 3 vols.
Religion and the Rise of Capitalism, R.H. Tawney, John Murray, London.
Islam and the Theory of Interest, Dr. Anwar Iqbal Qureshi, Idarah-i Adabiyat-i Delli. Delhi, India. Reprint 1979.
The Great Silver Bubble, Stephen Fay, Hodder & Stoughton 1980.
The Causes of The Industrial Revolution, R.M. Hartwell, Methuen & Co. 1967.
England's Apprenticeship 1603-1763, Charles Wilson, Longman 1984.
The Jackson Economy, Peter Termin.
Capitalism & The Reformation, M.J. Kitch.
The Jews and Modern Capitalism 15th-18th Century, Fernand Braudel, Collins 1982.
Economic History of Europe, Fontana.
The Age of Uncertainty, J.K. Galbraith, BBC 1975.
A Short History of Money, George Winder, Newman Meame Ltd. 1959.
An Economic History of Medieval Europe, N.J.G. Pounds.
History of the Protestant Reformation, William Cobbett. (Google Books: http://tinyurl.com/css7uo)

Paper Against Gold, William Cobbett. (Google Books: http://tinyurl.
com/clpxzl)
*Usury: Proof that it is Repugnant to Divine and Ecclesiastical Law and
Destructive to Civil Society,* Father Jeremiah O'Callaghan. (Google
Books: http://tinyurl.com/cfx2zz)

Philosophical Perspectives

The Aristotelian Analysis of Usury, Odd Langholm, Unversitetsforlaget
As 1984.
Groundwork of the Metaphysic of Morals, Immanuel Kant, translated as
The Moral Law by H.J. Paton.
Riddles of Public Choice, Times Higher Educational Supplement, 25th
October 1985.

General Theories on Usury and its Development

The Idea of Usury: From Tribal Brotherhood to Universal Otherhood,
Benjamin Nelson, University of Chicago Press 1969, an account of
usury based on the Deuteronomic commandment.
The Nature and Necessity of Interest, G. Cassel, Macmillan, London
1903, supporting the idea of interest and relating back to when it
was known as usury.
The Money Mystery, by Sir Norman Angell, Dent, London 1936.
Generally pro-usury.

Usury as a Subject in Literature

Collected Prose of Ezra Pound, Faber.
The Ten Symphonies of Gorka König, Ian Dallas. Kegan Paul. London,
1989.

Sex And Destiny, Germaine Greer, Secker & Warburg 1984, Chapter 'Fate of the Family'.

Popular Works

Cataclysm, William Clark, Sidgwick & Jackson.
Third Wave, Alvin Toffler.
Breaking Through, Walter & Dorothy Schwarz, Green Books Devon.

Academic and Professional Works Relating to Usury

The Scholastic Analysis of Usury, John T. Noonan, JR. Harvard University Press 1957 As its title indicates, in-depth with lots of references with a chapter (XX) on modern accounts. This is considered to be a standard reference by scholars.
Money, Whence it Came, Where it Went, J.K. Galbraith, Houghton Mifflin 1975.
The Making of Economic Society, Robert L. Heilbroner, Prentice-Hall Inc., Englewood Cliffs, New Jersey 1975.
The Money Market, Marcia Stigum, 2nd Ed. Dow Jones-Irwin 1978-1983. Homewood, Ill. USA. The classic educational text for participants in the money business. Takes usury as a given, while revealing the inside details of the actual trade in money.

Controversial and Rare Works Addressing the Issue of Usury

Lincoln Money Martyred, Dr. R.E. Search (pseud?) Omni Publications, Hawthorne, CA. 1985.
The Struggle for World Power, by George Knupfer, Plain Speaker Press.

The Rise of The House of Rothschild, Count Egon Caesar Corti. Western Islands. Belmont, Mass. USA 1972.

Films and Documentary Material
(Some Internet links are given here, although they can expire)

Concursante, Rodrigo Cortés' 2007 Spanish language film which, through the story of a man who wins the biggest prize ever in a TV competition, tells eloquently of the deception in modern monetarism, finance and banking.

America: Freedom to Fascism, Aaron Russo's 2006 film about the Federal Reserve Bank (a private bank) and the legality of the Internal Revenue System. (http://tinyurl.com/d7dosl)

The Money Masters – How International Bankers Gained Control of America, author Bill Still provides a great deal of historical data on the emergence in the US of the current financial system. (http://tinyurl.com/c6azry)

Money as Debt. Paul Grignon's 47-minute animated presentation of "Money as Debt" tells in very simple and effective graphic terms what money is and how it is being created. (http://tinyurl.com/ctdsyn)

Websites

The Open Trade Network is an initiative which seeks to restore the foundations and practices of a sane economy. (www.opentrade.org.uk)